# THE END OF THE WORLD
## and  what to do about it

A handbook for the practical idealist

*The Wm- sons...*
*The Best is Yet to Come!.*
*Love.*

# THE END OF THE WORLD
## and what to do about it

A handbook for the practical idealist

by
Hugh Jeffries and Leslie Fieger

A Justin Thyme Book by Alexander Publishing, inc.
North Hollywood, California, USA

**The End of the World**: A handbook for the practical Idealist
by Hugh Jeffries and Leslie Fieger

Copyright 1999 by Delfin International

Cover art and design 1999 by Lydia C. Marano

Published by Justin Thyme Books
a division of Alexander Publishing, inc.
13243 Vanowen Ave. #5
North Hollywood, California 91605

http://www.alexpub.com

ISBN: 1-893475-30-1

First Printing September 1999

Printed in the United States of America

Dedicated to

*Buckminster Fuller*

# Acknowledgments

The authors wish to acknowledge, with sincere and everlasting gratitude, the dozens of great Saints, seers and sages, mystics and mentors, teachers, gurus, scientists, poets and writers, philosophers and futurists, palmists and gypsy queens for their insightful thoughts over so many centuries, which the authors freely drew upon to form the basis of this book.

Deep appreciation is also sincerely given to all of the authors' friends and extended families for their profound skepticism, strongly held opinions, well-meaning criticisms and most of all for their support and unqualified love.

The information presented in this book reflects solely the authors' opinions and because almost everyone has an opinion about almost everything, the opinions expressed herein are no more and no less valuable or accurate than anyone else's.

Forward by Medard Gabel
  Ending the World as You Know It   **11**
A Prologue
  To The End Of The World   **15**
Introduction   **21**
The Last Chapter   **31**
Y2K=Y2K + 1   **45**
Human Evolution   **53**
Quantum Belief   **61**
It's All in How You Look at It!   **71**
The Sky Is Falling!   **83**
Evidence of Life on Earth   **89**
A Different Chapter   **97**
Waking the Sleeping Giant   **107**
Artificial Intelligence,
  Artificial Respiration and
  the Great Paradigm Shift   **117**
I Got Your Self-Awareness!   **139**
A Visit to Camp Nirvana   **149**
The Ins and Outs of It   **157**
What To Do About It   **167**
In Defense of
  the Way Things Are   **177**
The Next Chapter   **183**
So What's Next?   **195**
About the Authors   **201**

# Forward by Medard Gabel
## Ending the World as You Know It

There are many ways of dealing with the future.

You can ignore it.
That seems to be popular.

You can be overwhelmed by it.
Even more popular.

You can believe that everything is going to be alright: you are one of the chosen people. Most every religious faith has this buried somewhere in its catechism.

You can try to be clever and predict it. There's a lot of folks doing this. Some even make money from it, successful stock analysts and gamblers, for example. Some gamblers and stock analysts find their inability to predict the future to be frustrating, even bankrupting. Another group of people, futurists, economic forecasters, government prognosticators, and fortune tellers, have developed techniques that range from trend extrapolation, scenario writing, computer and role playing simulations and Delphi techniques to crystal ball gazing and palm reading in their attempts to predict the future. Some, in the hands of a skilled practitioner, actually work—in the short range.

There have been many proclamations throughout history about the end of the world. They have all been right. They have also all been wrong. The world does end for us, on a personal basis. Every night when we go to sleep, we *end*. Luckily, most often, we wake up. We also die. Eventually. The End to life as we know it, at least. The "world is ending" shouts from the rooftops are always wrong if they attempt to include anything more than the shouter's personal world. The world does not end on a cosmic basis. It keeps moving along. It's just a tad bit egotistical to think something that has been around for billions of years is going to choose the infinitesimally brief time we are around to take its curtain call, make its grand finale, and PUFF! disappear, maybe with a bang, maybe a whimper, but surely, on our watch.

Other than ignoring, believing, and trying to predict the future, you can try to create it. Or as Peter Drucker says, "The best way of predicting the future is to invent it." This more proactive approach appeals to those who do not like to sit by as passive observers of their fate, but who like to participate in the on-going evolution of their lives.

Russell Ackoff has said that, "The inability to envision a positive future is, in itself, a threat to survival." If we think the world is going to blow itself up in two months or two weeks, why not engage in self-destructive activities? Why not shoot up heroin or drink and drive? What difference could it make? Or, on the public policy front: James Watt, the former Secretary of the Interior under Ronald Reagan, was a firm believer that the Second Coming/Apocalypse was just around the corner and used this as a rationale in his attempt to sell off virgin growth timber resources in National Parks. "They're all gonna be gone soon, why not sell em off now, when we can git some benefit?"

The future is not to be predicted, it is to be planned. The future is not to be believed, it is to be created. The future is not a passive playground for the disaffected or terminally nonchalant, it's the place to actively engage our sense of responsibility for the things we do not like in the present and invent the world of our dreams. We need to all end the world as we know it and create the world we want.

This book may be a challenge for some, a stretch for others. My more serious scientist friends might be put off by some of the claims, but they will be wrong to disregard this book. This book can help you envision, imagine, plan, create, invent, and to participate in the future of your choice. Let it stretch your perspectives. Read it and laugh. Read it and rejoice. Read it and plan. Don't worry, participate.

# A Prologue
# To The End Of The World

Millennium madness! The growing frenzy surrounding the start of the new millennium has brought out all sorts of opinions, beliefs, legends and myths about the end of the world occurring some time about now. While most are preposterously far-fetched, many aren't. This book examines most of them and synthesizes them into an exciting preview of humanity's coming attractions. It takes into consideration a great deal of religious, physical and metaphysical evidence which is supported a growing number of experts who are now saying the end of the world as we know it really *is* going to occur some time around now when seen in the perspective of the 17.8 billion year history of our universe since the so-called Big Bang.

The writers maintain that when the information is considered cumulatively, it validates the notion that the end of the world as we know it is more than merely possible, in fact it's an impending probability. With the intention to inform rather than merely alarm or sensationalize, the authors provide even the most skeptical naysayers with sufficient factual evidence to make their own decision. Once readers know what's so, they can then ask, "so what?"

The authors believe that those of us alive today comprise a chosen generation of the first-born 'children of the universe' where the designing intelligence of everything created humanity in its image as the first and only species ever given the awesome power to affect not only the course of its own evolution but its own environment, as well. And now the time has finally arrived for us to end our gestation period in the planetary womb and begin our journey out of Nature's birth canal. Processed through natural selection, all of humanity is now poised on the threshold of an entirely new and unimaginably wonderful existence. It is about to happen, but not before we pass through the most terrible times the world has ever known.

Whether we like it or not, the soon-to-be 'end of the world' we've all heard prophesied and ballyhooed is about to occur. It's sure to be a calamitous time ending with most of humanity propelled toward its manifest destiny—a magnificent new existence characterized by much greater freedom, a more far more complex order to everything, and a vastly expanded collective consciousness—or disaster. The choice is ours to make.

This book describes the three major forces driving the impending transformation of the human community into an entirely different existence and offers proof that the ultimate evolutionary imperative is about to enter all of our lives.

The authors' suggestions for what action to take are grounded in a brand of *'practical idealism'*; pragmatic, common sense actions readers can choose to follow for successfully negotiating this soon-to-be event in a way that remains consistent with most of their religious beliefs as well as with scientific facts and the natural order of things. Because the vision people have of themselves and their future plays an important part in creating that future, the authors try not to drive readers into a pit of pessimism and hopeless, helpless despair but instead offer time-tested, positively oriented solutions to prepare for what is about to be humanity's inevitable crossing over to the next age which the authors have labeled the Age *of Conscious Awareness.*

The authors peek into mankind's past both real and imagined, look hard at the state of the world today and then provide a glimpse into an extraordinary future of mind-bending possibilities. You will be entertained. And motivated. Most importantly, you'll discover exactly how to prepare yourself for what's next.

After the material in this book is objectively considered, the authors hope it leads reasonable people to conclude that preparing themselves for the 'end of the world' is definitely in their own best interests because humanity's ultimate destiny is coming straight at us. We are the deer in the headlights. Dare to imagine it! Ignore it at your own peril.

*Humans have less an idea of their ultimate destiny than a grain of sugar knows the destiny of a Snickers bar.*

*Anonymous*

# Introduction

I

To get a better understanding why so many people have recently begun to think it's possible that these really could be the end times, it's useful to put all of the evolutionary history that has transpired since the beginning of the universe into a reasonably accurate time perspective. With that in mind, try to imagine that you have inserted a very special kind of video into your VCR. This video will run at the usual 30 frames per second and you should be prepared for a very long story because it depicts most of the major points in the history of the universe since the so-called 'Big Bang' all the way up until now.

This unusual video compresses all the 17.8 billion years of universal history into one. The video starts exactly at midnight, January 1st, and will run every day, all day and all night, non-stop, until it finally ends precisely at midnight, December 31st, New Years Eve. One year exactly. At the end of this movie, you'll have a much better time perspective on how long humanity has been on earth compared to the time that's passed since the Big Bang. So, load up on popcorn and kick off your shoes.

The tape starts and in the first frame, virtually in a nano-second, an explosion of unimaginable magnitude occurs. Nothing in science or language can adequately describe what happened in the first hundred millionth of a second. It was a state of pure energy, nothing but light. For the next half hour or so, representing thousands of millions of years, all we see are stable atoms of nitrogen and deuterium forming. Nothing else very interesting happens for the rest of the first month of our movie. The 'Big Bang,' so nicknamed as the beginning of the universe, was a supremely mysterious event with no apparent cause. Nobody knows what existed, if anything, prior to the Big Bang. So, with nothing very exciting happening on screen, maybe we can use the time to wonder exactly what it was that exploded. If nothing existed before the big bang explosion, then what exploded? And what caused the explosion?

Our video cranks along day and night and around the beginning of February, we see clusters of primordial galaxies forming into giant clouds of hydrogen gas and eventually they condense into the first stars. Some of these early stars generate so much heat and energy that we see them explode into monstrous supernovae, each of which is many times brighter than an entire galaxy. Easily the best celestial fireworks display of all time, these first thermonuclear explosions generate so much pure energy that they cause, or allow, nearly all the chemical elements to be formed and the force of these explosions propel the heavier elements far out into space. Tens of millions of years pass and we see them eventually condense into other new stars which then explode again in majestic brilliance. This spectacular process continues to repeat itself over and over again in our movie all the way until September rolls around. And, because our movie started in January, we're now eight months into our video and about twelve billion years have passed.

It's right around now that experts say our own sun was formed as a fourth generation star. It was out of these giant space furnaces that the earth's chemical makeup was permanently fixed for all time. This is why scientists have been able to prove conclusively that virtually every thing on earth, every single atom, was at one time or another processed through a star. This means that the earth and every living thing on it, including every human being who ever lived, was literally created from stardust.

Now we begin to see some serious action in our movie. Scientists tell us that our own solar system formed some time around four and half billion years ago, somehow materializing out of a cloud of frozen hydrogen and helium. But the earth was unique from all the other planets because it contained a powerful diversity of all the elements required for life. Exactly how life itself began remains a topic of debate but the experts all agree that life's essential compounds formed shortly after earth's birth.

As our video rolls along all day and all night into October, it's about three and a half billion years ago and we start to see the simplest cells forming. It's unlikely that those initial cells survived for very long. Life likely emerged many times over only to be consumed again and again. Eventually life in its simplest form, algae and bacteria, evolved. That life wasn't so simple, as we shall see.

Now comes a long, rather tedious period in our movie while these bacteria continue to very slowly evolve. It's a good time to make more popcorn or take a long nap because this process takes about two weeks in our video or several hundred million years in real time. Instead of breathing oxygen, these bacteria produced it as waste. This was enormously significant because among other things, it points out the exact time the earth's first pollutant was born. That's because oxygen at the time was a thoroughly toxic, deadly poison to all other living things on the earth. We'll talk more about that crucial development later.

After about another month or so of watching our movie, oxygen begins forming into a very thin layer of ozone covering the earth in a kind of protective cocoon, acting as a kind of shield from the deadly ultraviolet light of space. It was exactly now that an incredibly important design innovation was desperately needed if life on our planet was to survive because certain pollution death for every living thing was at earth's doorstep in the face of this deadly new poison called oxygen. Back then, if you couldn't process oxygen, you were finished, kaput, wiped out. However, just in the nick of time, innovation won out! Incredibly, the things that were alive began to adapt to this new deadly killer. A miracle if there ever was one! A terrible predicament of Nature turned into a huge opportunity. Oxygen continued to build up, bacteria began emerging that could not only tolerate the poisonous oxygen, they thrived on it! Voila! Aerobic organisms. And life was saved!

Then, about one and a half billion years ago the oxygen got to a concentration of about 21% and it suddenly stopped. It's now around the beginning of November in our video and things begin to speed up exponentially. Simple cells, which as it turns out weren't simple at all, begin to be integrated with other ones creating much more complex cells and then suddenly, we get to see the very first examples of reproduction. Sex! Wow, what an idea! The inventions called water and oxygen were fantastic ideas but this thing called sex was a really big leap forward because it permitted all sorts of different adaptations to spread very quickly. This new development catapulted the pace of evolution forward into an even faster mode.

It's now early December and we've been watching this video for eleven months now. Most of the movie is behind us but the evolutionary process of life on planet earth has just started and human life is yet to begin.

We see the next giant evolutionary leap happening now, in the first week of December, about a billion years ago. It turns out the new cells didn't have enough food to continue feeding themselves properly. They had reached their limits to growth. They were stymied and their life appeared finished. If they couldn't figure out how to transform themselves into something new, better and different, their time had come. They had to either change or die. There were no other options. Disaster was imminent. Oh well, nothing that ever lived was designed to last forever and their time had come. They had reached their limits to growth. Too bad.

But wait! Evolution had a brilliant solution. It was putting a limit on how big the cells could grow. This caused them to somehow cling together, which allowed them to continue growing in different ways, resulting in the creation of larger whole systems. Surprise! The first multi-cellular life emerges and very smart cells they are, too. These much better and different cells also had separate job descriptions. They specialized, adapted and innovated. These very clever cells even figured out a way to replace the other cells as they died off.

So now it's the middle of December, about 600 million years ago. Our video continues to motor on, 24/7 when suddenly we see a fish plop out on dry land and start flopping around. Nothing like that had ever happened before and pretty soon we see more complex multi-cellular organisms showing their faces. Now we're in the last week of our year long video. This continuing acceleration process is now picking up even more steam and is racing forward at a pace that seems out of control!

Giant dinosaurs dominate the landscape for most of the last week of our video up until around December 30th, about four hundred million years ago. We see a volcanic eruption so powerful it splits apart the giant land mass and kills off 80% of everything. Now it's about 200 million years ago and we see the Atlantic

Ocean forming between the two drifting land masses when all of a sudden ... ZAP!!! A huge, fiery asteroid plunges into the earth around the Gulf of Mexico. The giant dinosaurs disappear almost instantly.

Now, it's just a day and a half before the end of our movie, about 65 million years ago, and things are getting really frantic. Plants begin to wildly sprout up all over the place and different animals, now with plenty of food to eat, soon follow. The pace of evolution ramps up even more and everything rockets forward at an ever increasing, breakneck speed. How long can this keep up? If this goes on much longer, something's got to give. It can't keep ratcheting up faster and faster forever!

The video continues rolling along into the late afternoon on the very last day of our movie, December 31st. Suddenly we see man's earliest relatives show up. And now it's New Years' Eve, only about an hour or so before midnight. Our 365-day and nightlong movie is almost finished. At about a quarter to twelve we see early man stand upright on two legs. Now there's only two minutes left in our movie. The speed keeps increasing even more as human language begins. With only sixty seconds remaining, farming starts. With just ten seconds left, Buddha sits under the Bodhi tree and achieves enlightenment. With just two precious seconds remaining a man calling himself Jesus appears telling everyone the Kingdom of God is at hand and everyone should prepare themselves for it.

In literally the next single second the fall of Rome, the Dark Ages, the industrial revolution and both world wars whiz past. At last we're down to the very last frame in our year long film. One thirtieth of a second is all that's left and it zips by so fast we couldn't even see that it contained everything that's happened on earth in the last 50 years. The tape comes to a stop. The movie's over.

*All history moves toward one great goal.*

James Joyce

# The Last Chapter

Most stories have a beginning and an ending. But our story, the story of humanity, is still unfolding. Humans are an unfinished work in progress so many people aren't sure if we're in the early stages of our own story, somewhere around the middle of it, or close to the end. Nevertheless, we do have some excellent clues to help us decide.

Could it actually be possible for us to know our own destiny? When we consider what is known about Biblical end time prophesy - as well as the voluminous writings from history's saints, sages and mystics, and proceed to combine all of it with hard scientific knowledge from our 17.8 billion year evolutionary history, it appears to be possible to predict with a fair degree of accuracy if and when this world as we know it shall 'pass away.' Of course, it's not possible to know exactly when the final day will come but the evidence is in and the facts clearly point to the end times occurring sometime very soon, in our lifetime, like it or not.

Predictions abound. Even the architects who designed the great Egyptian pyramids flatly announced the world would come to an end just as they believed it did before. Only this time it will be in September 2001 at the end of the 12,500 half solar year cycle. The ancient Egyptians were no dummies! Neither were the Celtic Druids who said the end would come sometime during the year 2000. The great Chaldean philosopher Berosus predicted way back in the second century that the world would end abruptly in October of the year 2001. Nostradamus wrote that the end of this age would begin on July 1st, 1999. Add to that list of esteemed people Brigham Young, Helen Blavatsky, Mother Shipton and many others; add also the Australian Aboriginals, and the Incas. There is also an overwhelming amount of biblical prophecy saying the end times are upon us. This coming 'change' is predicted to be far greater than an 'age change' which experts say occur about every 2000 years or so and are always accompanied by an enormous shift in human awareness delivered to the world by an Avatar. The last age change was marked by the appearance of Jesus of Nazareth.

Millions of Judeo-Christians believe biblical scholars who quote God's words saying 6,000 years had to pass before the reappearance of the Messiah, Yahweh, Jehovah or God by any other name. The year 2000 marks the end of that six thousand year period - after taking into careful consideration the various Gregorian and Julian calendars that made no distinctions for B.C. or A.D. dates. Other biblical experts are quick to point out that until recently very few of the many end time prophecies in the Book of Revelation could possibly have made any sense until the Jews returned to Israel 50 years ago. Everything's now in place, they say, for the time of the end and to ridicule the idea is the height of uninformed, egotistic foolishness.

We know that humanity has not been around very long on the cosmic calendar but by whatever means we use to measure the passing of earthly time, it's of little real consequence to exactly when we can expect the end of the world. Neither does the new millennium have any significance other than for the first time in history, nearly everyone on earth knows it's coming. A thousand years ago, most people didn't even know what year it was.

In some cultures the year 2000 passed a long time ago. The Jews count from the 'moment of creation' which the bible says was 3760 years before Christ. The Hindus count from 3102 B.C., the beginning of the Kali Yuga time cycle.

The Muslims measure time in lunar cycles and using an Islamic calendar, the year 2000 won't happen until 2562. The Mayans use cycles of 5200 years and according to their calendar the world will come to an end during the next cycle that begins in 2012.

It is well known that our own calendar using the birth of Jesus Christ as year one is inaccurate in light of the fact that Christ was actually born between 3 B.C. and 5 B.C. In fact, it was only about 1400 years ago that a monk living in Rome came up with the system of counting from the year Christ was born and this calendar system didn't come into worldwide use until the late 1800's. So it's safe to say that the onset of the third millennium isn't a date that by itself is significant especially since the great cathedral of time doesn't even exist as we know it in God's infinite universe.

Nevertheless, calendars are a very significant source of valuable information because they measure a lot more than just the passage of time. They also record what's happened in the past and they can also predict future events very accurately within fixed and measurable time periods. The Mayan calendar, for example, is based on the 26,000 year cycle of our solar system gathered around the Pleiades star system. It calculated exact solar flare cycles, the precession of the equinoxes and even the ultimate rise and fall of their own civilization. Their calculations were so precise that only recently have scientists been able to equal their exactness using sophisticated solar observation satellites and advanced computer technology.

We humans can witness many different cycles in our own lifetimes. The 24 hour day/night cycle, the 28 day cycle of the moon, the 365 day cycle of the earth around the sun and the 28 year cycle of sunspots. Other cycles we can't witness because of the vast amounts of time they take—like the return to earthly view of many known comets. Cycles have a measurable effect on all kinds of behavior; the moon, the tides, female periods, seasons, climactic changes, solar flares and genetics, the sun's magnetic field fluctuations and the earth's magnetic changes. Easter, for example, occurs the first Sunday after the first full moon following the vernal equinox and it's different each year because of a particular celestial cycle. This is a very significant fact because the celebration of the resurrection of Christ, as well as our own rebirth and eventual transformation into a new and higher order, is also based upon celestial cycles which point directly at such a happening occurring soon.

The precession of the equinoxes works the same way. In a complete precessional year there are 12 divisions or zodiacal signs, four equinoxes and four seasons, which impact virtually every issue that's relevant to human survival. The earth is now fast approaching another equinox and very dramatic changes are unavoidable. Scientific evidence supports the many legendary tales of a massive geologic disturbance about 6,000 years ago, which changed the world forever. It also suggests another major earth change took place about 12,000 years ago. In fact, evidence found in Egyptian pyramids report that all of civilization suddenly disappeared at exactly that time.

However, believing in a time-certain date for the ending of the world is difficult for any rational person to swallow. Making a serious attempt to predict exactly when something so dramatic is going to happen is supremely unwise. All calendars, however useful, are really just human inventions. Furthermore, no less an authority than Jesus said that no man, not even He, knew the exact time of the end. In that respect, it's interesting to recognize that up until now humanity has been acting out biblical prophesy almost exactly according to the Word which, if nothing else, is a living testament to the everlasting applicability of scripture.

The bible was written by about forty gifted people as a highly complicated, fully integrated system of communication which contains hundreds of very straightforward predictions accompanied by thinly veiled clues about the coming end times. Two thirds of everything in the bible is about the future, including a description of the terrible 'fear and trembling' which the tiny city of Jerusalem will soon bring to the entire world. It is to come at a time when all the world's governments rise up against Israel and 'unless these days are shortened' by the re-appearance of the Messiah, all of humanity will perish in a conflagration the likes of which the world has never seen. "As in Noah's time, so shall it be."

Many biblical scholars assert that virtually every major theme of biblical prophecy has now been fulfilled, the most significant of which was the return of the Jews to their homeland in 1948. Gog and Magog, the re-building of Babylon, present day political plans for a one world government and even a one world religion, the re-building of the Temple in Jerusalem, worldwide moral decay, wars, more earthquakes, crimes of hate and prejudice, the doctrine of demons, death worship, gangs and satanic cults, children disrespecting parents, 140,000 abortions each day all fit with end time prophesy more than ever before in history.

The bible predicted the end times would witness the magnificent greening of Israel's dry desert land. Today, when seen from space, Israel looks like a giant fertile oasis surrounded by brown deserts. The world has come to see the day when Israel fills the world with fruit from its parched earth, just as the bible said it would in the last days. Nowadays Israel sells flowers to Holland!

But why tiny, ancient Jerusalem? It has no resources, no seaport and it's not militarily strategic. It does, however, represent the national identity of the Jewish people, which they've maintained for thousands of years and it's this which is the fundamental key to all of biblical prophecy. No other people in history who were scattered around the world have ever maintained their identity without having a country, however, the Jews have done exactly this for thousands of years, and even a million Hitlers working together could never successfully eliminate them. Jerusalem is now and ever shall be the center of our world, a perfectly focused eyepiece through which all of humanity's future can be seen. It's also the foundation of the world for the Christian, Muslim and Jewish religions.

Ancient myths, substantiated theories, various legendary hypotheses and religious teachings about the end of the world fill volumes. However, our world has been functioning for over 4.5 billion years so if such a thing was even remotely possible, where's the good, hard scientific evidence to give it some credence? Upon careful examination, there's far more scientific evidence than there is spiritual proof about how and when the world could end. The possibilities, in fact, are almost endless.

The end of the world could easily result from either a geologic or magnetic polar shift. Because the earth revolves on its own axis like a spinning top, it wobbles around just a little. Near its bottom is a glacier two miles thick and bigger than all of Europe. It's growing at the rate of 500 billion tons a year and it could cause the earth to start acting like an off-center load of wet towels in a clothes dryer, easily knocking the rotational center of the world off kilter. It's happened before and there's plenty of geological evidence to prove it. So, if this gigantic hunk of ice, which is thicker than 90% of the mountains in the world are tall, continues to grow it will cause the earth to topple out of its present rotation causing huge earthquakes, giant tidal waves, and hurricane force winds. Worldwide massive volcanic eruptions will spew billions of tons of ash into the atmosphere blocking out the sun and darkening the skies. Suddenly we have a new ice age on our hands and most of civilization would be destroyed.

Alternatively, a massive piece of ice called the Ross Shelf could break off at any time and be quickly pulled towards the equator by the earth's centrifugal force where it would melt, causing ocean levels everywhere to rise over 100 feet. Since most of the world's population lives less than 100 feet above sea level, the world and all of us in it would be up to here in deep trouble, to say the least.

An unusual alignment of other planets and their gravitational pull could exert enough force to cause the earth to undergo a massive polar realignment causing the earth to literally do a flip-flop. Normally, planets are spread around the sun so the gravitational effect of one is offset by the others. However, once every 6250 years a maximum pull is exerted on the earth by the rare alignment of the Sun, Moon, Mercury, Venus, Mars, Jupiter and Saturn all on the same side of the earth. This unusual configuration could off-set the earth's normal gravitational pull. The next time this unique planetary alignment will occur is May 5, 2000.

Magnetic polar shifts offer us another possibility. They've occurred several times as a result of the earth being struck by a giant asteroid. Even a near miss can cause a change in direction of the earth's rotation from clockwise to anti-clockwise. A shift in the earth's magnetic pole wouldn't destroy the world but would confuse the bejabbers out of literally every living thing. Birds would forget to migrate. People would be totally disoriented and their body clocks would go on tilt. Whales would lose their sense of direction and all things technological or otherwise would suffer from a weird type of severe dizziness. Nothing would be left unaffected.

However, the most critical concern lies within our own sun and the changes taking place there. The sun's magnetic field is not as simple as earth's whose two poles act like a stable magnet. By comparison, the sun's three magnetic fields are definitely not stable. Instead they move all over the sun's surface and its interior. From time to time a perfect, neutral magnetic balance is reached and when this happens, the magnetic field can suddenly and unpredictably reverse itself. When and if this happens, the earth must instantly realign its own magnetic field to be in sync with the sun's. Many scientists say this is what probably happened about 12,500 years ago and again

6250 years later. Either a geologic or magnetic shift occurred and either one could occur again at any time.

The peak of the next solar cycle begins in January, 2000 and is expected to last into the summer. The latest data from NASA points to the very real possibility, and some say probability, that the sun is about to go through one of these magnetic polar shifts. The coming sunspot cycle is anticipated to be stronger than any yet recorded which might knock out many orbiting satellites and upset the earth's power grids. In an attempt to study this problem NASA plans to launch a new satellite in late 1999.

In the meantime, a more realistic gloom and doom death warning for earth can be found much closer to home. Our planet is spinning around in a veritable shooting gallery of more than 2,000 mountain-sized asteroids, any one of which could end it all if it struck the earth. Over a thousand of them measuring more than a half-mile wide now intersect the earth's orbit. In June 1996, an asteroid more than a third of mile across came within the moon's distance to the earth. That's a near miss according to experts and you don't even want to think about an object of that size smashing into the earth at 70,000 miles per hour! Even more worrisome to scientists is that asteroid appeared out of nowhere, virtually undetected and was discovered not by some government watchdog organization but by two University of Arizona students scanning the skies one night. Such an object hitting the planet could jar the earth's tectonic plates out of their relative geologic quiet and trigger massive earthquakes.

Astronomers tell us such a collision on the west coast of the U.S. would at the very least sink the east coast of America in a giant temblor. New York City would submerge and the shock waves would flatten everything in most of North America, cutting off the sun and sending the temperatures plunging below zero. No place in the world would be left unaffected.

If a large meteor or comet hit anywhere on earth it would certainly threaten all of civilization and every living thing. They also promise one or more is sure to strike the earth at some time. How much damage it would do depends upon its size but even a medium-sized one would cause the earth to stagger and wobble around. Shock waves would rattle everything from Mexico to India, totally upsetting Nature's equilibrium, causing volcanic explosions and a long cosmic winter. And forget about trying to shoot any asteroid out of the sky before it hits the earth. Scientists say we're a long way from being able to do such a thing.

The world could also end by ice. Experts say that one day another ice age will definitely occur and remind us it was one of the environmental changes which divided Homo sapiens into the different races 100,000 years ago. Large parts of the world would be covered by a mile thick blanket of ice making it very cold and hard to grow things, to say the least. Other doom and gloom possibilities include supernovae raining down lethal x-rays to earth, killing everything alive. Such supernovae occur about every 500 years. Experts at Caltech tell us they'll give us plenty of warning if any nearby star is about to go supernova providing they happen to be looking there.

In the meantime, how about we puny humans setting off a chain reaction from some kind of economic meltdown, religious uprising, or political squabble leading to war? Could anything man-made be powerful enough to actually precipitate the beginning of the end of the world? It's not impossible—we are certainly capable of precipitating an uncontrollable thermonuclear chain reaction, either deliberately or by mistake.

*The world is far too dangerous for anything less than Utopia.*

Buckminster Fuller

# Y2K = Y2K + 1

**1**

Nowadays human problems like the Y2K computer bug are serious dilemmas that need handling. A trillion dollar repair job, Y2K's impact will be felt in every industrialized country in the world and could have an impact far beyond what most think or are prepared for with disruptions perhaps fomenting a domino affect jump-starting a series of testy worldwide problems. With tens of billions of microprocessors imbedded into everything from human heart defibrillators to airliner fuel systems, Y2K's a serious concern but it's very unlikely to create an end of the ages scenario. Besides, most of the rest of the world isn't even computer reliant, so there's no need for us to scamper off to the mountains with a year's supply of toilet paper and Spam just yet. Y2K will eventually pass without causing the beginning of the end although it may be riding shotgun. If you're an opportunistic lawyer, you might even find yourself catapulted straight into litigation heaven.

And how about some kind of catastrophic third world conflagration triggering the end of the world? After all, the great Red Menace in China continues to be a festering sore with a hundred million man army of young men holding hundreds of armed nuclear missiles. A severe shortage of women in China, a result of a cultural bias against the value of females compounded by an ill-conceived government solution to over-population, has left millions of horny young men with their hormones raging and little, if any, chance of coupling with the opposite sex. This has historically made young men very cranky and anxious to fight, a fact not wasted on China's aging communist leaders, still yearning for revenge against the Japanese for their treatment in World War II. China's not fully computerized but they're known to have created a powerful arsenal of viruses to use in screwing things up for any nation who is. Many in China think a war with the United States is inevitable and probably will involve Israel. So, while the Chinese are definitely a danger that needs careful watching, they're not likely all by themselves to trigger the end of the world. If they do, they'll probably get plenty of help from the Americans.

How about an out of control dictator or a starving and desperate country dragging other more powerful allies into the ultimate, massive earth-ending conflagration? Perhaps a fractured former Russian empire erupts in civil war and it spreads like a virus, sucking other countries into it. Maybe part of the old Russia gains control of strategic weaponry, gives up its civil wars and ethnic cleansings, and marches on Israel with Arab or Chinese help, with America coming to Israel's defense? That would be BIG trouble and while anything's possible, all by themselves each of these are improbable end times causatives although they could certainly accompany it. A tragically sad and massive die-off on the African continent also falls into this category.

And we also can't ignore the pure economic time bomb that is the worldwide fractional reserve banking system that is fomenting global money problems in every hemisphere. Huge, politically charged national debts or the squirrelly derivatives market, could belch up unimagined troubles for a global economic system which is already creaking under the load of a fiat monetary system based entirely on 'agreements' about the real worth of currencies—virtually all of which have now been debased to the intrinsic value of the paper they're printed on.

Meanwhile millions of capable people all over the world are scrambling about because of currency fluctuations, downsizing or rightsizing and the ever-expanding mega-mergers. On a daily basis, economic myths about personal job security are exposed worldwide for what they are, and people everywhere are being forced to virtually 're-invent' themselves regularly merely to survive as the global economy shifts from the industrial era to the information era. Personal opportunities are forsaken, careers ended, and with every passing day doomsayers are blowing optimism to kingdom come—asserting even our health and safety are at risk with mutating incurable viruses evolving all over the world. They say terrible economic signs of the end times are everywhere and we should see them as scriptural signposts pointing us all toward a very displeasing and soon-to-be end of it all.

Then again, China might decide to move on a now defenseless Japan, simultaneously grabbing Taiwan while tightening its economic grip around the throat of free Hong Kong. Japan would look to the U.S. for help. If refused, they could call in the billions of American debt they're holding. Again, unimaginable grief but probably not world-ending.

And what of Europe's new European Union? Most Christian Bible scholars see this as the long-awaited re-birth of the Holy Roman Empire. When it and NATO eventually collapse they'll point to those events as prophesied precursors to the end of the world.

So, as the cosmic clock strikes 2000, everywhere we look the world is up to its adenoids with ongoing economic, political and religious problems. The growing list of problems seems intractable, as does a long list of ecological urgencies, wars and rumors of war and growing biological terrorism in a world that seems to have lost its moral compass. The U.S., having self-appointed itself as the world's policeman, not surprisingly also has the world's largest prison population and has seen it double just in the past ten years. As the U.S. continues trying to legislate morality, it teaches everyone they're not really responsible for their actions and in the process infantilizes an entire nation, which only insures more of the same.

And finally, what about a liberal dose of old-fashioned political shenanigans leading some powerful leader to start acting irrationally—arbitrarily starting a war that triggers the end of the world? Not likely but politicians can sure be expected to create lots more government red tape, more illogical laws, bigger government programs and much higher taxes as bureaucrats worldwide continue to be myopically more concerned with things physical than with things spiritual. Don't be surprised if people who smoke need a prescription to buy tobacco while others are required to answer to the government about the fat content in their diet. More and bigger government, in its futile attempt to create ever-increasing orderliness in society, is typical of the human condition and it fits exactly into many biblical experts' end time scenarios.

It also fits perfectly with the on-going, natural evolutionary process.

*For we wrestle not against flesh and blood but against principalities, against powers, against the rulers of the darkness of this world and against spiritual wickedness in high places.*

Ephesians 6:12

# Human Evolution    2

When we look at various scientific and man made possibilities for the end of the world, together with the well-known spiritual prophesies, metaphysical predictions and a long list of ancient legends, they explain, or at least make it understandable, how a growing number of people are becoming thoroughly convinced the end times are upon us. It's unwise to pretend all the evidence doesn't exist and it's impossible to remain ignorant of scientific facts, much less unlearn what we already know. Neither can we stop learning about the accumulation of empirical facts, which validate so many age-old promises. Still, dedicated skeptics continue to discount them, while believers say that the world can now be sure something that's been foretold for thousands of years is about to happen. Although many other generations throughout human history also thought they were living in the last days, as we inch into the third millennium, the evidence keeps piling up to now convince even the most confirmed doubters that a dramatic sea change is coming at us and it will be a truly momentous shift in our paradigm.

Scientific facts prove that when great evolutionary shifts take place, they're of such a sudden and tremendous magnitude that they leave behind giant missing links similar to what happens when water becomes steam. The old is totally disappeared and the new, while containing evidence of the old, is so dramatically different from what it was that it's virtually impossible to see how the new ever came out of the old. If we examine the caterpillar closely we find no evidence of the butterfly it will soon become. Likewise, dissect a butterfly and we'll find no traces of the caterpillar it once was.

Perhaps most significant, when the evolutionary process produces newness, it is always characterized by three common traits: a much more complex order, far more freedom, and vastly higher consciousness. That's the nature of Nature. The evolutionary process always works toward producing higher consciousness and history proves it. And what about all the terrible things we see every day in the form of man's inhumanity to man, the violence, the wars and the endless unmanageable troubles in the world? Are they historically consistent with the evolutionary process? Absolutely yes.

Unworkability and breakdowns are a necessary part of evolution and we can expect even worse in the future. We should plan for the pace of life to continue speeding up, with everything getting more and more complex, with even worse troubles until an eventual limit is reached. At that point a complete and total change, a veritable transmutation must take place within the global human community or humanity will die off. That's the way evolution works. The evidence is crystal clear. Really terrible, intractable crises have historically always preceded momentous evolutionary breakthroughs. In fact, they are a natural and necessary precondition to all major changes. They represent one of the major forces that drive the entire course of evolution and transformation. They also explain why the grief and strife we see around the world today are not deadly evolutionary mistakes but natural and very necessary parts of our growing up as a species. Painful as they may be, they're all part of Nature's selection process. They are fundamental not only to humanity's maturing but also fundamental to everything in all of Nature.

The truth is, every single thing ... all the good and all the bad ... that has ever happened in the history of the world happened exactly the way it was supposed to happen and to prove it, it did. All of us are part of Nature's own on-going selection process as we travel along on our own evolutionary journey, learning the lessons of the differences between good and evil.

Whether we want to believe it or not, the evidence points to the certainty that all of humanity is about to undergo a gigantic leap into the next stage of its own evolution and this coming change will be accompanied by, among other things, a leap forward in consciousness so great none of us will even remember this mortal life. We will evolve to a new and higher order or die off. Like other monumental evolutionary changes, it's certain to be punctuated by a sudden, calamitous and even apocalyptic occurrence every bit as dramatic and historically significant as when the first fish, one day billions of years ago, jumped out of the ocean and started flopping around on some deserted beach.

People like Moses, Jesus, Buddha and a tiny handful of others 'found out' about life on this plane, learning about the next stage in human consciousness.

They did their best to describe what the next level would look like, giving it names like Heaven, Nirvana and The New Jerusalem. Others called it Valhalla or Elysium Fields. Hard as they tried, their well-meaning attempts to provide us with a glimpse of our own destiny has somehow always seemed incomplete because our immature minds can't fully grasp it. Soon, however, we will. We may have no choice.

It's only recently that science has provided us with powerful, new ways to look into our past, enabling us to see the future with unprecedented clarity. Soon we'll come to know not only how we may pass into the next level of human evolution but also when. And, while it's unlikely to occur next week or next month, Nature clearly has it penciled in for us some time soon. Perhaps a year from now, perhaps five or maybe ten or twenty but in any case, sometime right around now in the cosmic scheme of things.

And exactly what will the changeover process look like? We can be certain it will be so dramatic and incredible that when it's complete, the world as we know it will have become virtually unrecognizable. Nothing will be the same. Humanity is about to give birth to itself. We're all traveling down Mother Nature's birth canal kicking and screaming and fighting among ourselves like the selfish, self-centered, narcissistic creatures that we are. Soon, however, we will all be called upon to fully cooperate in the process of moving ourselves out of the birth canal and into the unknown. Those who don't cooperate, we will surely die while the those who do will move on as the process of natural selection continues its endless work.

Humanity today is like a newborn baby born into a universe that's probably teeming with life and doesn't know it. We can't see it and like all newborns, we're just beginning to learn. We're like a baby in the crib whose newborn system isn't fully coordinated yet. Like the baby reaching for the rattle and missing, we're not quite completely wired up and fully operational. As a species, we're not yet fully mature because we haven't been around long enough. Our collective nervous system, the ways we now communicate, are not yet mature, not yet working synergistically and evidence of this can be seen all over the world. Millions of souls cry out in pain and despair while others don't even hear it, can't hear it and therefore don't respond.

This is because of several factors, one of which is all of humanity is stuck in it's own self-centeredness. We have not progressed past our infantile narcissism. Furthermore, despite the message historical Jesus gave the world, most people have only recently begun seeing their connectedness to one another and begun realizing their interdependence with other humans. Beyond that, more and more people are recognizing their relationship and interconnectedness with the earth itself and the impact their behavior has on our common home, planet earth. Up until the atomic bomb, humans didn't think that any of their activities could possibly affect the world's basic operating system in any meaningful or lasting way. Today humanity is learning to see things very differently.

One day soon all of humanity's nervous system will become fully hooked up and on that day, synchronous thoughts will emerge on a mass planetary scale.

Unprecedented miracles will occur. As a result, each part of the human planetary body will quickly begin functioning synergistically in perfect synchronization. We'll be like the baby grabbing hold of the rattle at first try and shaking it. That day will be upon us very soon and when it comes all of us will open our eyes and see our sameness, our connectedness. At that magical moment the entire planetary human body will naturally begin thinking and behaving as one living, comprehensive organism. That day is nearly here. It is imminent and unavoidable and all who can intuit such an event should be preparing for it.

And what will the next world look like? Answering that is as futile as a flower bulb trying to imagine the radiance of its coming bloom. Or our simple garden caterpillar friend trying to imagine itself as the butterfly it will soon become. It's simply not possible to sketch an accurate picture of what the process of transformation or the end result of the next stage of human evolution will be like. One thing's sure; it'll be very interesting. All we can do now is learn from the wealth of scientific and spiritual information that's available to us, try to imagine it, expect it to occur and prepare ourselves as best we can.

*Behold, I shall show you a mystery!*
*You shall all be changed, in the twinkling of an*
*eye.  This mortal flesh will become immortal*
*and death shall have no dominion.  The suffer-*
*ing of the present cannot be compared with the*
*glory which shall be revealed in us.*

Corinthians 15:52

# Quantum Belief

3

Every culture in history has its own strongly held beliefs about the end of the world, giving strength to the theory that mankind invented its own doomsday. Others say all the preposterous speculation about the end times being upon us is cheap brainwashing, about as reliable as advice from a psychic hotline. The Hebrew prophets, in fact, never did predict the future, saying man's free will determined his own destiny.

But other pre-cognitors, sages and seers, serious philosophers, theologians, clairvoyants, mystics and even some palm readers and crystal ball gazers have been pulling on their chins thinking long and hard trying to foretell the end of the world. In the process, many have managed to scare the living bejabbers out of millions of gullible, albeit well-meaning people with their 'sky is falling' routine.

Millions of people on earth today hate thinking about the various end time scenarios or any talk about a life beyond this. They say all it does is squander thought energy; it's a stupid topic that's not only boring, it shouldn't even mildly engage any normal mind. It's a waste of time, a big downer and anyone who thinks about end of the world possibilities is a badly damaged nitwit. Not only is it irritatingly dull, all it

does is foment arguments. Besides, they say, if the end
of the world does come, so what? What can we do
about it? We'll all be dead anyway, snuffed out like a
used cigar. Afterlife talk is all bull. Next we'll be
hearing about the tooth fairy.

People who think this way resist, defy, withdraw
and ridicule any possibility that humanity is now on
the threshold of discovering life after this one and how
we can learn to become partners in the overall process
of creation. They refuse to take responsibility for
their own growth. They refuse to dream even though
dreams are free. They remain ignorant that dreams
are the very thing the world runs on. They argue that
learning to expand one's spirituality doesn't benefit
society as a whole but only the individual and therefore avoids the real issues facing humanity. They say
the entire human potential movement as a whole is
basically anti-social and all religion is merely an opiate
for the masses. They ridicule those who are interested
in either one to give up their inner journey of self-discovery and spirituality and deal with more pragmatic
things. They argue that most people involved in both
religious instruction and the human potential movement are far from being enlightened themselves, but
instead are detached and preachy, and act as if they
know something others don't. They say they're hypo-
crites and are more concerned with their own
thoughts and desires than in doing what works for
others.

What most of these people don't realize is that the
discovery of one's inner spirituality and self-knowl-

edge is profoundly rewarding, the richest type of fulfillment there is and it's largely unavailable in the external world. Once awakened to their own spirituality and expanding awareness of their inner self, these people might cast aside their ego-centered needs long enough to discover true self-fulfillment, lasting self-satisfaction, and a happier, healthier life.

For most people, the idea of the end of this world and a transformation into another is merely a pathetic dream sequence that can't possibly happen. But what if these same doubters somehow came to know beyond any doubt that the end of the world was imminent? What would they do? In all likelihood, people would be divided between those dropping down on their knees, repenting and crying for salvation while most of the others would probably surrender to their dark side in a last ditch effort to 'get theirs.' As a result, any earthly semblance of law and order, civil safety or kindness to others would be abandoned, quickly leading to total entropy. Riots, stealing, killing and looting would take over, and a complete breakdown scenario much more terrible than anyone's worst dreams would ensue. Living all their lives in a 'get' world, those people would be too hardened to adapt to a 'give' world.

How much thought have most rational people really given to the possibility, however farfetched, that the final curtain could be rung down on us? If they did believe it, what would they do about it? Collapse down on their prayer bones and start taking hot laps around their rosary beads, hammering out a salvation plan for themselves? If the bible is to be believed literally, it looks absolutely hopeless for us, because it says we have to alter our behavior, which is like asking human nature to change. And just how is humanity expected to pull that one off? Everyone transform themselves? Love others like they love themselves? Are you kidding? How? Human nature just isn't capable of changing itself all by itself. Or is it?

Perhaps a good place to start is for each of us to ask ourselves if we can continue to afford the arrogance of living our lives as if we've got all the answers. As if there's nothing worth knowing that we don't already know. That's a fatally flawed mindset, especially when we discover that the knowing of certain facts could completely transform the quality of our lives.

It's valuable to know, for example, that each passing day sees more scientific and spiritual evidence validating the truth that creationism and evolution are sympathetic and largely congruent with each other. And despite what some extremists profess, quantum mechanics, time and space physics, expanding universe reversal, imminent cyclical completion and the process of evolution all support the coming end of this age and are in perfect sync with biblical prophesy. It's important to remember, humans did not invent evolution, it invented us. And God, by whatever name, created it all.

Everybody also thinks evolution is a very slow and gradual process and it's true. However, it's also periodically interrupted by gigantic and unexpected leaps forward. These leaps forward, so great they leave no trace where they came from, creates 'missing links.' This explains why scientists seldom find fossils showing a smooth, logical evolutionary progression but instead they dig up fossils for one species and then others that followed them proving that one evolved from the other. However, they find very little fossil evidence showing the bridge carrying one to the other. This is because there usually isn't any. Scientists tell us these sudden, giant evolutionary changes were once separated by billions of years, then millions, and then thousands.

Meantime, the evolutionary process continues to accelerate faster and faster each day, constantly speeding up and now trucking along at what seems to be an out of control rate with no indications of slowing down. We've also learned that missing links are a natural part of the evolutionary process and at first seem unexplainable, simply a gap leading to a dead end.

If we think about it, each of us also experienced a similar type of evolutionary leap in our own way when we successfully passed through our own Mother's birth canal. We had reached a point of limited growth in our Mother's belly and we either had to drastically change our way of life and our environment or else we'd have surely died. Somehow, without any instructions, we had no choice but to be birthed. We didn't know how to do it, there wasn't anybody who could tell us how and even though we did have some outside help, we accomplished it mostly all by ourselves. In the process we created our own kind of missing link. Even the memory of our own birth has been blocked out and it wasn't that long ago. We remember nothing of where we came from.

Whether we realize it or not, each of us has somehow been imprinted with the know-how for figuring out for ourselves how to evolve into a new and higher form without any instructions. We also know that the birthing process is very dangerous and when we finally do evolve into a new and higher form, we can expect our payoff to be far more freedom, much more complexity and a vastly higher consciousness. It is these three characteristics which are always consistent with how Nature works. Throughout the entire process we can depend on being guided by the same irresistible, unseen power that is attracting us.

Everybody also knows that the birthing process, once it starts, cannot be stopped. If fetuses could talk they'd tell you they never expected such a thing to occur and made no plans to be born. Yet one way or the other, we all did it and in doing so, discovered that we accomplished a crucially important thing without being taught. Can we presume from the birthing experience that when we really need to know how to do something critical to our survival, we'll know how to do it when we need to? Is it instinctive to know the really important things in life? Things that can't be taught to us ... like how to be born, how to walk, how to breathe, how to wake up?

It appears that all of mankind is on a physical and

spiritual journey through time in search of its own origins and is constantly attracted by some invisible power. Could we also be a species with a kind of amnesia which has until now kept us condemned to looking into our past in search of our future? Like trying to drive a car through the rear view mirror, we wonder why we have trouble navigating and then, just in the nick of time, we'd turn around and faced forward, be made fully aware.

Evidence of past evolutionary 'triggers' which caused all of the momentous events since the Big Bang explain why the present times signify a great deal more than our simply attaching importance to some arbitrary calendar change. This is due at least partly to a growing consensus that's rapidly spreading around the world, suggesting a true inter-connectedness between all people as well as an inter-connectedness with our common home, the spaceship earth.

More and more people worldwide have come to realize that humans along with everything on earth constitutes one giant living organism. The earth is at last being seen for what it truly is, a living, breathing organism in its own right. Humanity is just now finally awakening to its ultimate role as a kind of central nervous system for the entire planet.

*The earth is now passing my window.*
*It's about as big as the end of my thumb.*

Neil Armstrong, Astronaut

# 4

# It's All in How You Look at It!

Try to imagine yourself standing on the moon. That spectacular blue and white, pearlescent marble dominating your view is earth, your ancestral home. It's about four times as big and five times as bright as the moon and it contains almost everything that you care about: family, friends, all things alive and all things fun, art, music, religion, history, food, sex. Standing on the moon you stare slack jawed far into the deep blackness of space. It is deafeningly silent. Without the cloudy atmospheric haze that impedes your view from earth, you're bedazzled by millions of stars shining far brighter than you've ever seen them before. Your mind boggles at the inconceivable hugeness of space.

All the stars you can see make up less than one billionth of the known universe. Your precious earth is part of a galaxy called the Milky Way, which contains 100 billion stars. And there are over ten billion galaxies! Some experts say there are over 1,000 planets in our galaxy that could support life as we know it. Looking at earth, you see the outline of the North American continent and realize that if all of the United States and Canada together represented the size of our galaxy, the entire solar system would be about the size of a single walnut located inside it. The size of earth would be less than a single pinprick, just less than 1/10,000 of an inch in size.

Looking at Mother Earth from the moon, you begin to realize that it's more than just where you come from. You also get a sense that you're part of it and all humans as well as all living things on it are an integral part of it. You have the same thoughts that have occurred to many who have visited the moon; could it really be possible that the earth is one giant living organism in its own right? From the perspective of the moon it certainly looks like it may be. And why not?

More and more people are now seeing the earth as a living organism both physically and spiritually, seeing it as alive and like them with a type of soul, a genuine emotional and etheric body. Seen from outer space, the earth has an aura of energy much like humans. It is certainly divine in its nature. It was conceived and born in an instant flash of time while the sun was in the sign called Aries. And even though the sun sign of earth is Sagittarius, some astrologers tell us another planet will one day very soon accept the karmic responsibility of supporting life in this solar system and they point to the sign of Sagittarius, the centaur, whose arrow goes far out into space directly toward the mathematical center of our own Milky Way.

We have come to know that the questions and answers about the origin of the universe and everything in it rest upon the cornerstones of both science and theology. Few of us are yet accustomed to thinking of the earth as a living organism, much less as something with moods or feelings or emotions. Yet if we skeptically allow ourselves to see the earth that way, we begin to recognize weather patterns, tsunami, volcanic explosions, earthquakes and other events as possible evidence of those kinds of human characteristics. Can we believe that it may be possible that our planet is affected by an unrecognized force exerting its influence on us? It's hard for any rational person to accept this notion because our intellect calls for reason and logic rather than something so flimsy. It requires tapping into our intuition which is a much higher form of mental activity. Intuition is spiritual in nature and therefore eternal. Spirituality, in fact, is the only part of us that is always immortal.

And can the earth likewise be immortal? We all know the earth is organic, so could it be like us, in a manner of speaking. If so, the earth and all of humanity are eternally linked together in an evolutionary process of ever higher and higher consciousness. With our ancestral home's variety of spectacular topography, we see something certainly every bit as alive and vibrant as any other organism. Past civilizations have thought the earth was conscious; the Native Americans, Sumerians, Egyptians, Mayans and Aztecs understood a greater sense of the earth's ineffable presence, and they left copious writings and drawings to prove it. Native Americans even constructed their religion upon honoring the entire earth as being alive and fully aware.

However, opening the minds of people the world over to the notion that the earth is a living thing rather than a lifeless rock floating in space is an idea that's hard to sell because it carries with it such enormous implications and personal responsibilities.

Nevertheless, the earth continues hard at work preparing itself for the next phase of its existence while millions of people all over the world are doing the same for themselves. The earth, like humans, has a mysterious internal mental capacity of some kind that now lies dormant, quiescent yet pulsating in its own rhythm, waiting for exactly the right moment to reveal its aliveness. It's in our own best interests to look upon our earth as a living and continually evolving home with its own cosmic personality, unlike so many other planets, which appear so unwelcome and uninhabitable to us.

The day has thankfully come and gone when most people took our planet for granted. Indifference to the earth has changed radically and we are witnessing a tidal wave of ancient and modern, scientific and spiritual prophesies about coming earthly changes. Many of these prophecies are now verifiable, comprising a strange cross-pollination of ideas. Increasingly, we see man functioning in a manner that contributes profoundly to the ultimate destiny of the planet. And even though the scientist and the Sunday preacher, the philosopher and the agnostic approach the subject from disparate angles, they ultimately all arrive at the same conclusions: Man clearly plays a much more important role in his own destiny and the destiny of the planet than was ever previously imagined.

You stand on the moon staring in amazement at the sparkling, beautiful earth. It's infinitely more inviting and attractive than anything else you can see in the heavens, silently hurtling through space at 35,000 miles an hour with its special atmospheric safety blanket protecting all living things on it. Truly a marvelous sight to behold, it supports untold trillions of living entities. It seems to live and breathe just like all other living things with its own pulse, night and day. The rivers, the tides and the oceans take in nourishment and cast out waste much the way your own body functions, acting like the earth's giant circulation system. All the while, the trees and vegetation take in carbon dioxide and give off life sustaining oxygen for you to breathe in the never-ending process of photosynthesis.

If the earth really is a living organism then it logically follows that all things alive on earth must be part of an enormously complicated, perfectly balanced ecosystem. You know the earth somehow has the unique ability to self-regulate all its conditions as well as the composition of everything needed to create and sustain life. In fact, everything on earth somehow learned how to mysteriously come together for one common purpose; to create, to protect, to preserve and expand all life.

Amazingly, the earth's surface temperatures, according to scientists, have remained nearly the same for hundreds of millions of years. The earth's oceans have forever maintained their same percentage of salt. Life-giving oxygen has been stabilized at an optimal balance and a very tiny amount of ammonia in the air

is exactly the right amount to sustain and preserve
life. The climate and the chemical properties of the
earth are absolutely ideal for life as we know it, and as
far as we know, in all of the universe, the earth is the
only planet configured the way it is. None other has
an ozone layer in the upper atmosphere shielding it
from deadly rays that would otherwise kill off the life-
giving molecules. Your very own earth certainly is a
miracle! And you're an integral part of it.

Could it all be simply a consequence of a series of
fortunate circumstances, an unimaginable combination
of unlikely accidental flukes? The GAIA hypothesis,
on the other hand, implies that the entire biosphere is
a single living organism, very carefully organized bio-
logically to sustain a particular environment and it's
very much a living entity in, of and by itself. Therefore, when you consider the earth and the entire biosphere as one living organism, it seems sensible to also
consider yourself as an integral part of that larger
whole system. How can you not be an integral part of
it?

General Systems Theory postulates the world is
one monstrous, organized hierarchy of inter-related
energy and matter. As such, nothing can be considered on its own because everything is part and parcel
of a complicated set of interacting systems making up
a larger, more complex whole system.

All things, therefore, are composed of many sub-
systems that take in, process, and then expel energy
or matter. Just like the human body, planet earth

takes in and uses and then excretes oxygen, all of it functioning within a mind-boggling degree of predictable internal order, despite dramatic environmental changes taking place all the time. If we think of the biosphere we live in and the planet we live on as a singular living, interrelated system, then how can we legitimately separate ourselves from it? The fact is, humans may be the single most unique ingredient in the entire delicious recipe, because we're what gives the whole thing consciousness; and higher consciousness, which includes the survival instinct, is a constant and never-ending evolutionary goal.

So you stand there on the moon and begin to pridefully take some small credit knowing you are a part of it ... like a tiny living cell in an unimaginably enormous and complicated nervous system. You imagine trillions upon trillions of messages continuously flashing about on the earth's surface, like a massive planetary web, as everyone goes about doing their thing—discovering more about themselves, their consciousness and their planet. From this you begin to sense the power everyone on earth has to consciously affect their own future.

Suddenly you remember the story of the flea that one day jumped off the elephant it was living on and looked up at it to realize for the first time that its host, the elephant, was alive! Wow! The elephant's a living, breathing thing! Forever after, that flea never again would look at the elephant the same way.

You realize that the one constant, overarching

belief in all the world's religions is an acknowledgment at the most profound, fundamental level that all humans are of the same essence as each other and of everything in the universe, stardust! You know deeply that all people are tied together as one at our core. In fact, the word religion means precisely that; tied together at a common source. We are not all separate; at the core we are all really one, a notion that remains rock steady as humanity's deepest level of its own identity. This is why if we carefully examine and analyze a single snowflake we see it's made up of the same essence as all the others, and yet it's totally unique. And so it is with humanity and with all the rest of nature.

It's this sense of sameness that is a fundamental principle of all religious teachings and traditions. Even different phenomena in the farthest reaches of the universe have been proven to be manifestations of a single fundamental whole system. Called the 'perennial philosophy' by Aldous Huxley, it's scientifically provable. All of us are composed of only a hundred or so various types of atoms and literally nothing else. Every single thing on the planet including the earth itself was processed through a star. All of us were and everything was created from pure stardust!

So, while Mother Earth operates in its own Gaia consciousness, chugging along on its evolutionary journey, humanity is now becoming more aware that it's not simply hitch-hiking along. Humanity is also becoming more aware of its responsibility for functioning as a kind of central nervous system for the planet, acting as its global mind. More and more people are beginning to see the earth this way ... that it's a bonafide living organism in its own right and humanity's job is to serve as the earth's own consciousness mechanism, its planetary brain, if you will.

This type of collective thinking is consistent with the evolutionary process because the ability to see the bigger picture and to understand a larger context is also part of evolution's constant goal of creating a higher consciousness. So, to put a positive spin on what many feel is an event to be feared, the fast approaching end of world should actually be seen as an incredibly exciting opportunity. It's good news! In fact, nothing could be better. Especially if you're ready for it.

*Nature has only showed us the tail of the lion.*
*I have no doubt  the lion belongs to it*
*even though he cannot reveal it.*

Albert Einstein

# The Sky Is Falling!

# 5

And what could trigger the end of the world as we know it? Pragmatically, we know humans probably don't have the capacity to trigger the end of the world by ourselves but we do possess the capability for intuiting what's in our own best interests. And most of us could certainly use some divine guidance to cast out our self-centeredness long enough to consciously help ourselves get successfully rebirthed into a new and higher order. And that's exactly what's going to happen. In order to move to the next higher level of our own evolution, each of us will have to give up our own self-centeredness. That's a very tall order! Just how do we do that? Only God, if you believe in God, has that answer and He may be holding His breath waiting to see if we pass the test. Remember, our species was never guaranteed it would survive forever in its present form and furthermore, it's in the natural order of things for species to become extinct. So the jury's still out on whether humanity will pass or fail the ultimate exam that's in store for us any time now.

From what's known about the end time prophesies, it seems to be in our own best interest to spend some time and energy exploring the various ways to prepare ourselves for what's next ... emotionally, physically, psychologically and spiritually. Being aware and ready for the next stage of our own evolution makes good sense and the very first step should be to learn how to be more spiritual, how to develop a higher personal consciousness of mind and better know ourselves. We should begin working right now to recognize the emergence of our own divinity and the role each of us plays in the unfolding saga about to be revealed. In the face of an evolutionary shift of the magnitude that's in store for us, it makes perfect sense to know what we can do to affect our own transition. We need to realize that we have the capability to consciously self-design who and what we shall become individually and collectively. We need to know without any doubt that it's our own thoughts that will actually create our future. And since we're in charge of our thoughts, we're also responsible for them, and our own future. To get ready for the next phase of our evolutionary journey, we should be in our best possible physical condition because our future will be affected by everything we do and say, everything we think, even by the kinds of foods we eat.

Many people will scoff, even ridicule these suggestions while others will respond when it's too late with a lame, reactionary knee-jerk response in a last second survival attempt. But Nature doesn't care. Its own process of natural selection never stops and with every passing day some people are self-selecting themselves in while others are self-selecting themselves out. That's the way evolution works.

Biblical end of the world predictions say 'the earth shall pass away" and the end times will be punctuated by a horrendous apocalyptic event, culminating in a final judgment day. The bible says if we don't have the essentials of our salvation firmly in place, we've got zero chance of getting past the pearly gates. Most doomsday scenarios carry the same admonishment; either we change our behavior or else. Highly respected religious teachers have even said we've got it coming to us; we're really asking for it if we don't or won't alter our bad behavior. This is both an admonishment and a very serious threat. Humanity has been told to literally transform itself and if it can't, the final event, the end of the world, will be our deserved penalty. They say God wants everyone to move onto the next level with Him and He will make it available to virtually everyone in what would have to be the biggest, grandest and most interesting come-as-you-are party of all time.

The so-called end of the world does not necessarily mean the end of all life on the planet. The world will continue on either with or without humanity, much the same as an elephant continues on after some intelligent, self-aware flea jumps off. The world will indeed continue on without end, but all of its inhabitants won't. That will depend upon the way they think.

*The millennium is a state and stage of mental advancement, going on since time ever was.*

Mary Baker Eddy

# Evidence of Life on Earth 6

The shift into the third millennium has provoked lots of hand wringing for some people, even though it's an event that's meaningless to all parts of the universe except mankind. The last time there was a millennial shift, when the calendar moved from 999 to 1000, millions of people acted very strangely then, too. Thousands thought the end was nigh. The Vikings and the Russians converted to Christianity. And most futurists who accumulated large followings past or present in every culture predicted some time around the year 2000 or 'right around now' would mark the true end times. Significantly, most of them also believed there was little, if anything, that could be done about it. It was going to be an ugly doomsday, for sure. We'll all die in fire and brimstone, whatever that is. However, many also said that those who would be lucky or unlucky enough to be alive in the end times could save the earth and themselves by changing their un-Godly behavior and repenting. Personal salvation has always been a very powerful motivating factor for many people and it still is.

Teachers of scripture, psychologists, psychiatrists and your friendly local therapist as well as those in the human potential movement, specifically in the field of personal transformation and the anatomy of the mind, tell us people can indeed change. They insist it's possible and offer plenty of supporting evidence. However, they warn, there's a hitch. A major problem is it can only happen at the rate of one person at a time! One mind at a time. Just like in all religions, they say enlightened transformation can only occur at the level of the individual. It's not a group thing. Since the days of Moses the evidence is clear that seeing 'the light', knowing personal transformation has never existed at the level of any group or any organization. It's for individuals only. In fact, never in history has there ever been even one transformed organization. Not even one family. This makes enlightening one mind at a time a monumental and time-consuming job.

If you're one of those who suspect the end of the world might really happen, what are you doing, if anything, to prepare for it? Plenty of people say our ultimate destiny is pre-ordained, a pre-determined fixed part of our future. We can't change it or us. But they'd probably shudder with goose bumps if they knew about all the scientific proof that squares with much of that type of thinking. Plenty of metaphysical myths and ancient legends agree, too. But wouldn't an event of such astounding finality suggest to most pragmatists that it would have to have some kind of cause? But what? We know that everyday human activity is probably not powerful enough to trigger it, but what about an unstoppable super-natural force? Some unseen power that's been operating in us and through us forever? Something we've never thought about that would validate religious beliefs, legends, mythology and modern science?

There is a growing consensus rapidly spreading around the world that we are now living not just at the end of an age, but in the next few years a giant evolutionary leap forward will precipitate itself on a scale that hasn't happened in millions of years. And it will not come about as the result of human activity. There is a far more powerful force in operation and it is virtually unstoppable.

From every perspective we examine, if a new paradigm of existence does indeed emerge, we know that it must affect all of humanity because that's the way it works. We will all be born anew and no one will be left out. Those who are selected out will have somehow failed because of their own selfish actions and their own free will decisions. They will either be stillborn or remain on earth, while the others who made the grade will get to move on.

The planet will *not* disappear altogether, but many people certainly will in the single most unique event in the history of humanity. We get to live through it and the signs are all around us that it will happen soon!

Some people mistakenly think before the end actually comes that we'll have plenty of time to simply migrate to another planet. They're positive the ultimate fate of humanity must lie in the stars. But despite what's seen as ordinary in the movies, interstellar space travel is a supremely difficult task. At this time, the notion of warp speed is beyond anything but a sci-fi writer's wildest imaginings. And while it's a known fact of quantum physics that the earth must certainly one day die and humans must then leave the planet or die with it, that event is not scheduled to happen for about 5 billion years or so.

In the meantime, it's well known that as many as 10,000 planets exist in our galaxy which could support some kind of intelligent life. The truth is, the universe might be teeming with intelligent life. We just don't know it nor have we located another planet with life-sustaining conditions like ours. Until now, no one has found any sign of it, not one signal of sentient life detected even though for the past 50 years our planet has been emitting radio and TV signals so that and any planet within 50 light years of earth would be able to detect them, presuming they could. Would they respond if they could? If they happen to be thousands of years ahead of us scientifically, spiritually and tech-nologically, they certainly already know about us and maybe what they've observed hasn't convinced them that any really intelligent life on earth exists.

Religious teachers throughout history have been in strong agreement that trivializing end time prophe-sies would produce very grim results for anyone who mocks God's word. Others say that predictions of any end of the world scenario signaling the coming of the Messiah would cause only grief. So, the next apparent step for humanity to take in its own development seems perfectly consistent with our evolutionary his-tory. Everywhere we look more  and more people all over the world are now focusing their attention on inward spiritual growth, reaching in every direction for higher consciousness, learning more about themselves, nurturing their spirituality and becoming increasingly self-aware. More and more people all over the world are now recognizing they're on the threshold of the next phase in the ultimate creation of a universal super-organism of vastly higher consciousness. Many experts in the field predict before long a sufficient number of individuals will have been transformed or will be in process of being transformed. A so-called critical mass of higher consciousness must occur. Humanity will then be as prepared as it can be to move into its next stage, *the age of conscious awareness.* At that magical moment it will then become clear to everyone that our entire evolutionary history was intelligently organized and guided in a way that throughout the ages encouraged all living systems to continuously evolve in a never-ending cycle from ashes to ashes and dust to dust, always moving toward more freedom, increased orderliness and an expanded higher consciousness.

It's critically important that we humans realize that what we can and will ultimately become as a species is predicated upon our individual and collective awareness. The collective vision we hold of ourselves and for our journey toward whole-centered beingness is tantamount. We are the living actors in the greatest cosmic drama ever told, we're an unfinished species with unprecedented choices about our future. Virtually everyone is deeply involved in this unfolding, never-ending drama, whether they know it or not. Most, however, don't have a clue. Even so, no one can leave in the middle of the process whether they like it or not. They can no more opt out of this life than a single unaware cell in our bodies can flee from the game it's in. Nobody gets to quit this evolutionary game because we're all in it together.

Perhaps the biggest defining difference between any of us will be how each of us reacts to what the future brings. Very soon, we will learn how the organizing intelligence of the universe will communicate its plans to individual humans making up the larger holistic body. Those who can 'hear' the message will immediately intuit what to do. Those who can't hear or won't listen, won't. Not to worry however, Mother Nature is more concerned with the evolution of the whole rather than any of the individual parts. Therefore, it's important to practice listening very carefully. Spend time alone meditating, praying. Try to become better in everything you do and say. Learn to trust your intuition and nurture it, especially if you're a male. Soon we will all be re-made into *Ultrahumans*.

*Everywhere on earth at this moment,*
*in the new spiritual atmosphere created by the*
*knowledge of evolution,*
*there floats in a state of extreme mutual sensitivity,*
*a love of God and faith in the world;*
*the two essential components of the Ultrahuman.*

*These two components are everywhere 'in the air'*
*and sooner or later*
*there will be a chain reaction.*

Fr. Teilhard de Chardin, S.J.

# A Different Chapter

A French Jesuit Priest and philosopher, Pierre Teilhard de Chardin, long ago suggested that some day all of humanity would unify into one, interrelated, interdependent body. He observed that humanity had successfully passed through the first evolutionary stage, what he called geogenesis, the beginning of the earth and the second stage, biogenesis, the beginning of life. Now, he says, we're about to enter the next stage, which he called noogenesis, the beginning of the mind. Higher consciousness. He said this stage would earmark the climactic end of the evolutionary process, a veritable Omega Point, where we will be at one with our Maker and at last have revealed to each of us how to use not just 10% of our brainpower but all of it in an existence far beyond either planetary or individual consciousness. Father Teilhard described something that's not just a more, better or different kind of existence but something literally unthinkable, totally ineffable and virtually unknowable; an idea with the unique capacity to exist in the total absence of any accurate or even adequate worldly description.

Another great philosopher, Indian mystic Sri Aurobindo, interpreted evolution as Divine Reality saying that we shall pass from pure energy into and through solid, living matter to a higher consciousness. At this time in our history, he said, we're all about to be transformed into what he called Supermind, a level of enlightenment beyond anything we can even hope to understand, an all-embracing level of enlightened beingness, a fully integrated, all-inclusive planetary consciousness much like a kind of designing global intelligence.

Nearly a thousand years ago, an intellectually gifted Hopi Indian prophet named Massaw was highly revered among his people as a protector of the earth. He had many followers both within and without Indian culture and to them he gave a set of sacred Hopi prophecies that included 100 predictions for the future. To date, over 80 have come true and many are strikingly similar to those contained in the Bible. Massaw even saw the future invasion of his sacred Indian land by the white man 400 years before Columbus mistakenly bumped into the North American land mass. Massaw was truly uncanny. He foretold the invention of today's modern automobile as well as the Second World War. As a highly respected Hopi sage, he also announced that humanity could conceivably endure horrific end time events but only if it adopted seven sacred religious practices: *Revere the environment ... Be self-sufficient ... Be happy, never angry ... Uplift others and never diminish them ... Resist temptation ... Reject materialism... Teach children respect.*

The Hopi believe we can attune ourselves to the universe and bounce our thoughts back and forth. Like most Native Americans, the Hopi are very spiritual. They know humanity's role in the process of evolution and their account of the beginning of the universe is simple to read and beautiful to understand. The western-most of the Pueblos, Hopi means 'peaceful'. They live today in the middle of the great Navajo Nation and are best known for their elaborate religious ceremonies. Like the Navajo, the Hopi tell a story similar to the biblical tale of the great flood and maintain that the Grand Canyon is the carved out evidence of it. The world, they say, is very unstable and fragile in anticipation of the expected great end time transformation.

The Hindu religion, on the other hand, speculates on the nature of deity, the origin of the universe and its relationship to Brahman, the universal soul. For the Hindus, Brahman is the virtual source of the universe from which everything comes and to which everything shall ultimately return. A presence that pervades all beings, for the Hindus, Brahman is the very essence of the complete and total wholeness of an entire fully conscious universe. The quality of life for Hindus therefore, is determined by the law of Karma in which re-birth depends upon behavior in a previous lifetime. Hindu teachers always reply 'neti-neti' (not that) when offered an explanation of what God is. Whatever anyone says it is, it isn't. If you can think it, that's not it.

The Hindus tell us that humanity's ultimate evolutionary destiny is to become a fully aware species of higher consciousness and attaining this state of mind will deliver humanity right back to its own beginnings from where it came and from where it all started, at one with our Maker. The goal of each Hindu's existence is to escape from this endless cycle of re-birth and death and eventually gain entrance into that ineffable state Buddhists call Nirvana. A full circle journey. What happens then is anybody's guess. Perhaps another Big Bang and the process starts all over again.

In any case, all religions are obviously a direct reflection of people's thoughts and if there's one thought that all humans have in common it's the desire to transcend whatever mental or physical state they may be in at any given moment in time. So no matter how good things may be for us, no matter how content or happy we might be, we somehow always imagine and seek out more and better. The human brain was engineered to be a 'high-seeking' mechanism, which can experience contentment but is never fully satisfied. In our heads there's always something more, something better and different. Everyone is being pulled toward a more and better 'something.' It's as if every human mind has a certain type of transcendent nerve which always wants to go beyond where it is. All of humanity seems to function from a fundamental ground of being called 'this isn't it.' It's more than just escaping from our present state of mind, because no matter where we're at emotionally, even when we're our happiest, that's not 'it.' There's always more. And just what is it that all of us are yearning for, being drawn to?

Could it be we strive to one day be at-one, united with our Creator? Is that what's attracting us? Suppose we transcend this state and succeed in getting 'there.' What will we find? What will Nirvana, Heaven or New Jerusalem be like? Exactly what is the unrelenting, continuous attraction, this unseen, irresistible pull that's been constantly tugging at humanity since the dawn of history, forever drawing us toward something?

Everyone has their own separate island of dreams chock full of mysterious possibilities. This is at least partially because of the capacity of the human brain to be aware of all the possibilities, however far-fetched. This makes the brain a very powerful and dangerous tool. Up until now in our development we've only figured out how to use about 10% of its total capacity; like an iceberg, 90% of our brains are unseen, submerged, largely unknown. Furthermore, the brain's full potential has never been adequately measured so we don't even know what we're fully capable of.

In the history of evolution the human brain has by far experienced the most rapid development. Nothing even comes close to matching the astounding rate the brain has evolved and matured in humans. And, despite being a very recent evolutionary event, the human brain has evolved to its present state in only the last million years or so, a mere cosmic heartbeat. Why? What caused this? Where is our developing brain leading us? Some respected scientists are now saying modern humans are deep into a mysterious process of self-creating a radically new brain circuit with a special capacity that allows for a condition of neurosomatic inner peace. They say its part of our natural evolution and is only now very slowly and painfully emerging, running parallel alongside our ancient mammalian brain circuits. Experts say those who can recognize and develop this new brain circuit will have developed the quality that will allow them to progress to the next stage. Those who don't ... won't. However, we all have it and it's available to everyone equally.

Meanwhile, each of us is somehow trapped in our own so-called reality that we unconsciously manufacture. We see everything in the world 'out there' and apart from us. When we meet someone with a far different reality than our own, we think they're certifiably nuts; we try to avoid them or worse, try to change them. It's been said that the people of the world are all islands shouting at each other over oceans of misunderstanding.

Of course, it's neurologically impossible for any two brains to have the same hard-wiring schematic. No way any two can be genetically the same so everyone moves through life in their own separate, very private, self-created illusion/reality. If somebody speaks bow-wow and the other person speaks oink-oink, both think each other is a bit damaged. Buckminster Fuller said our bodies (hardware) are merely short-term, puny carcasses while our minds (software) contain the entire universe and virtually everything is already inside our brains just waiting to be discovered by us. How did it get there?

It's probably inevitable that to some people this

sounds like nonsensical gibberish or feel-good, new age psychobabble. But these same ideas come up in every language, including mathematics because they reside within our consciousness, and both math and language are excellent examples of human awareness. To truly make a quantum leap in our awareness, a major shift is required. That happens only when we completely change our thinking. This is the only pathway anyone knows that can lead to discovering higher consciousness. However, few are very quick to choose it because it means first identifying and then giving up some very strongly held, incorrect beliefs.

However, in the near future we'll all be required to do exactly that. We'll have to change the way we see ourselves, the way we see the world, what we believe and the way we behave. This becomes much easier when we come to realize that who we are, what we are and the way we are is merely a very carefully edited collection of what we have instructed our brains to tell us. And most of what we think about most of the time is pure nonsense.

*Can God make a rock so heavy*
*He can't lift it?*

Anonymous

# Waking the Sleeping Giant 7

It's known that evolutionary events happen very slowly and inexorably over long periods of time until the organism ultimately runs up against some terrible trouble, a problem so big that it requires a complete transformation or else it dies. These intractable problems always entail some kind of limit to the organism's growth until it eventually finds itself cornered and must alter its way of operating. If it doesn't innovate, it dies. It needs to somehow puzzle out how to truly re-invent itself or else it will disappear altogether.

Evolution's major miracles have always required the passing of major tests. For example, we know that early organisms had to learn to breathe oxygen, a deadly poison, or die. No government agency was around back then to declare oxygen illegal, so every living thing had to learn how to process oxygen or go the way of the buggy whip. And it remains so to this day.

Either mankind figures out how to transmute into something entirely new or it, too, will disappear.

There's no arguing that one of the greatest and latest evolutionary leaps of major consequence took place with the development of the human brain's extraordinary ability to know self-consciousness. This was an event perhaps as important as the emergence of life itself and it's a very recent happening. There is absolutely no evidence that early man possessed self consciousness. Initially, humans were conscious and then were suddenly made conscious of being conscious! That's what separated humans from the rest of the animal kingdom because while other animals are conscious, they're not aware of it. This phenomenon has different meanings to different people.

There is absolutely no existing evidence that early man possessed self-consciousness. It's clearly a characteristic which has forever been identified as the most precious gift from the essence of the Holy Spirit and is probably considered that way because the latter cannot be understood without the former. Self- reflective consciousness, the ability to think in the abstract, allows us to not only experience the world around us, but also to experience ourselves as the context within which the entire world exists. When we experience ourselves and our world this way, it's like watching a movie of our life. We can notice how we look and how we act, as well as evaluate our own personality. When we view ourselves, our world, and our circumstances this way, we're better able to make distinctions about how we should behave. Self-awareness enables us to not only be part of our own movie; it allows us to be the star, the writer and the director. We get to create our own life movie moment-to-moment, frame-by-frame. Life is not a dress rehearsal. Every day we can make distinctions about everything and especially the way we react to various circumstances. Bottom line, self-consciousness enables us to function in a way that we think is most appropriate to our own circumstances and survival.

Being self-conscious allows us to notice that when we become upset, the main source of the upset is usually our own unfulfilled expectations. Most of the time we get upset because things didn't turn out the way we wanted; we had expectations that weren't fulfilled. We forget that we invent all of our own expectations. We posses the ability, with practice, to learn the secret of how to take pride in the way we behave when we have unfulfilled expectations. It's not easy, but everyone can learn to do this successfully and be better off as a result. The way we behave when things don't turn out the way we want is an accurate yardstick of how fully conscious we are and a good measurement of how highly evolved we are.

The fact is none of us can reasonably expect to move to the next level of existence unless and until we become fully conscious creatures able to control our emotions all of the time, not just some of the time. Self-centered behavior definitely will not work in the next stage of human evolution. From a purely evolutionary perspective, self-consciousness and the rapid maturing of the human brain is so important that we can realistically equate it with the onset of sexual reproduction billions of years ago; because since the instant that humanity became fully conscious of itself, it's been able to accomplish truly incredible things. And in just the next two years, the accumulated knowledge of the world will double, which means that everything mankind knows about the purpose for our existence, how our universe functions and our expected future will double as well. With instant worldwide communications, this information will be available to almost everyone, profoundly impacting the world, our individual self-image, our thoughts and ultimately our future. There's no telling what its full effect will be.

It can safely be said that the gift of human self-consciousness, coupled with the rapidly increasing knowledge of how the brain and the mind works, are not leading up to more of the same for us, they're leading us into the unknown.

Every human brain is like a sleeping giant. Nothing else has ever existed that represents greater wonder or complexity. With a virtually unlimited capacity, as vast as the billions of galaxies in our heavens, each human brain has within it more than ten billion thousand possible neural connections. To label the brain the most complex piece of machinery in the universe is at once accurate and a gross understatement. Nobel Prize winning neurophysiologist Sir John Eccles said the hair-trigger sensitivity and the ultimate capacity of each of our brain's thousands of billions of connections seems to be like "a machine designed to be operated by a ghost."

Because our brains evolved over millions of years, the brain has its own very unique type of archeology. Each person's brain is as different as their fingerprints. Still buried deep within our brains are tiny evolutionary traces of our former reptilian and mammalian brains. Each human brain processes information differently and regardless of a person's IQ, every person's brain is the most astonishing piece of protoplasm ever conceived, with a magnificent capacity so huge it literally cannot be measured. Every human brain is a mystical marvel. Today's intelligent tests can't measure how smart someone is, they only measure how someone is smart. Every single person is smart in some way. Why we were so endowed is a subject of much speculation. What will we ever use such a large brain for?

The most complex and complicated organism ever developed, our brains have been incorrectly compared to a computer. No computer ever devised can begin to match the capacity of the human brain, which has a capacity so large we haven't even figured out how we can possibly use all of it. Like a huge storage container that's 90% empty, it waits to be filled. Whole areas of our brains just lie quietly waiting to be used. But for what? We're going to find out soon enough.

Scientists can't explain why the human brain evolved with such a limitless capacity. But it did and it wasn't a mistake. It also gave us the ability to learn virtually anything. So far what it has learned best is survival but what else does our brain know? The answer isn't knowable, but certainly one purpose for living is to fully develop and utilize our brains so that we can ultimately become all we're capable of. We're all players in the most wonderful game ever invented.

The brain's miraculous capacity for self-consciousness carries with it the awesome capacity for us to help engineer our own destiny and even control our own environment. It has made us the first and only species able to rationally anticipate the consequences and make intelligent choices according to what's in our best interest. And the dizzying speed at which we're now evolving makes the head swim with all sorts of bizarre possibilities that might be in store for us in this lifetime and the next. Only because we humans became self-aware that we can think about an evolutionary leap so dramatic that we label it the end of the world. Then again, if humanity ultimately flunks out as a species, completely disappearing, the world will continue on without even noticing.

So, the question is, as we move ever closer to the cusp of the next stage of human evolution, what will be our limit to continued growth? What could possibly be in our future that could force humanity to be instantly transformed into something new, better and different or else face certain extinction? That facet of evolution, science tells us, always contains massive disorder and confusion, accompanied by enormous stress, resulting in many deaths. Breakdown always precedes breakthrough.

Whatever it takes, we can be sure humanity will somehow figure out how to survive. We were made that way. We're experts at survival and we'll do whatever it takes no matter how uncomfortable. When we look at human history, there's no arguing the enormous success we've had in the short time we've been around. We're all true winners! Every human is a real champion and it started before we were conceived.

If you think about it, every single one of us at one time was among several million other similar-looking, tiny sperms, frantically wagging our tails with all our might in a once in lifetime survival opportunity. We don't remember it, but we were in a competition that our life depended on. It was a life or death swimming race, an all out struggle to stay alive for every one of us. We had to win that race and be the first one to reach the unfertilized egg descending down our Mothers' fallopian tube or we'd surely die. We'd be flushed out, dead. We didn't know exactly why but we were supremely motivated, frantically swimming upstream as fast as we could, elbowing millions of fellow competitors out of the way. Survival of the fittest. Nature's selection process was hard at work and we knew we had to get there first. We knew there'd only be one winner so we paddled along as fast as we could, determined to get there first. And we were right! Because if we didn't win, we'd never have been born. Talk about a major win!

From time to time it's good to remind ourselves of what we all did. Each and every one of us finished first in that historic race against the most overwhelming odds we'll ever face and that makes each and every one of us a very big winner! Every person alive today and everyone that ever lived won that race and fertilized that egg, so every human is a true champion to be honored and saluted and celebrated. You don't get to be here unless you're a proven winner. What's more, our individual and collective futures promise even more and bigger successes and more honors in the future.

Wait and see! It's our destiny.

One day soon, hopefully before the end occurs, enough people will share a mutually recognizable transcendent vision, a message that will be heard by all who are paying attention, which will drop silently into the brain of each person in their own language. That single event will permanently alter humanity's perception of this so-called reality we're living in. It will be like a giant overshadowing cloud is suddenly lifted and we'll all see the sky for the first time. Until then we should all live obediently in 'the half hour of silence' which St. John the Divine described so aptly.

Of course, there's always the remote possibility that we humans will blow ourselves up, even though the overwhelming odds actually favor the opposite scenario. All the symptoms of societal breakdown and hatred that we are living in cannot be dismissed but they should be seen for what they are; signs of impending breakthrough. So, even though millions of unenlightened people with no moral direction continue to mess up their lives and misery pervades much of the world, eventual human success is highly probable. Humanity, therefore, is much more likely to evolve into higher coherence, than plunge into self-destruction, because the force that's been working for millions of years will soon reveal an unmistakable path for us to higher consciousness and increased spirituality.

*In the last days I will pour out my Spirit upon all flesh.*
The Bible

# 8

# Artificial Intelligence, Artificial Respiration and the Great Paradigm Shift

Science proves that the more complex any system gets, the greater its instability and the sooner it will evolve. The world is certainly highly unstable today and getting shakier by the minute. When it does collapse, it's much more likely to collapse into higher consciousness than into self-destruction, partly because humanity isn't stupid. We're not suicidal dopes. Survival is a big part of our nature and with some outside help, we'll figure out what to do. We humans are pretty smart. We've discovered how to create new life in a test tube. We've not only learned to fly, we've learned to leave the planet and return. We know how to harness the sun's limitless energy, how to successfully transplant organs, clone living creatures and even create entirely new living species. We're learning to explore the vastness of space and live in its cold, hostile environment or at the bottom of the sea. We're getting better at creating artificial intelligence. By any measurement we've been super successful accomplishing things that up until recently were reserved only for God.

We've unlocked the secrets of the atom, discovered

the mystery of molecules and invented the computer. These three significant events are monumental signposts driving humanity into the quantum revolution, the biomolecular revolution and the computer revolution. All three are important evolutionary drivers. We are well along in the process of understanding consciousness. We are discovering our potential to manipulate the forces of Nature, transforming us from being passive observers of the great cosmic dance of life to the choreographers.

Today, our computer knowledge doubles every few months with upwards of 100,000 people going on the Internet for the first time each day. The quantum theory has given humanity a detailed description of the essence and workings of matter and for the first time the ability to see and understand the matter around us. Bacteria have been recently discovered that can thrive in water temperatures above 199 degrees Fahrenheit that is well above the known limit for bacteria to live. This directly challenges known truths and allows us to imagine finding other life forms that don't require carbon, nitrogen or water. We stupidly laugh at the ignorance of our forefathers because nowadays we've discovered the freedom to think the unthinkable. However, all our efforts at improving life through material things have severe limitations.

Modern computers, transistors, lasers, bandwidth and x-ray crystallography are some by-products of the quantum revolution. Soon the complete human genome will be decoded and the world will at last have a precise blueprint for human beings. This carries with it many ethical and spiritual considerations, along with the awesomely dangerous power to manipulate life almost at will.

Modern science has now learned the basic laws of almost every discipline; the theory of matter and evolution, space-time and the genetic code and still, humans have not yet become grand masters of all they survey and we won't until the nature of human consciousness is fully known. The acceleration of science and technology continue to rocket forward with profound effects on almost everyone's standard of living. However in the future, brainpower and our creativity will be the key ingredients. Soon the engines of wealth and real prosperity for everyone on earth will be deeply rooted in the triumvirate quantum, computer and molecular revolutions. Before long microprocessors by the millions will surround us everywhere and with each passing day the earth is becoming increasingly intelligent. Today computers and robots can automate DNA sequencing, providing the world with a literal encyclopedia for all living things on the planet. And that's only the beginning. Nature's process marches forward as everything continues to speed up. Things also continually get smaller, more miniaturized. Scientists now say they'll soon be able to make actual working machines the size of molecules! The evolutionary beat goes on ever faster.

Continuous advances in the art/science of artificial intelligence, where we're discovering how to duplicate the neural patterns of the brain by computer, will soon see robots with more than just a hint of self-awareness and limited consciousness. Imagine machines actually able to learn from their mistakes! We already know how to clone living creatures and design new life forms. Soon we'll be able to engineer the virtual mental makeup of our children. Is there any answer to where all this is leading us? Where is it that Nature is egging us on to? It seems like we are caught in a process headed towards the ultimate creation of a truly intelligent, spiritually aware, planetary civilization. But is all this activity simply market-driven or is humanity being divinely guided? Or could it be some of both?

Soon we'll hold all the information contained in the library of Congress on a single microchip and recall any of it in a nanosecond. A hundred years ago it took a year to get a message around the world; today we do it almost instantly, a development that is an important key to our future. Rapid worldwide information exchange represents one of the most significant of all recent human activities; it allows for the real probability that very soon all of humanity can be linked up simultaneously, a development with unimaginable future implications that also happens to be a fundamental key driving humanity toward its next evolutionary goal. We humans are now very close to mastering how to instantly communicate synchronous thoughts on a mass scale. This is information processing at its finest and is perfectly consistent with the evolutionary imperatives needed to trigger pervasive global change.

The ability to instantly exchange information among the whole of humanity can be thought of as being akin to the nervous system of our planet. Like a baby's nervous system, the world's nervous system is almost but not quite fully developed and connected. Inevitably, it will be soon. As a species, we're like newborn babies; we're stumbling about because our different nerve endings aren't fully developed and communicating. Very soon however, the world's nervous system will be fully connected and when this happens, nothing will ever be the same again. Then the cells in one part of our planetary body will come to fully know their relationship with the cells in another part and they will learn their common purpose just like in our own bodies. When this happens, miracles of unprecedented magnitude will occur worldwide. It's a very important design innovation and part of humanity's overall blueprint. Expect it, look forward to it and make yourself ready to handle it emotionally.

The computer revolution overwhelmed us with its capabilities but the fact is, when all the bells and whistles are stripped away, computers aren't really much more than fancy adding machines. Like idiot savants, they lack common sense. Still, computers will soon blanket the world creating a uniquely vibrant, intelligent communication membrane covering the earth. Improved artificial intelligence will give us machines that can be taught how to reason with real common sense, be able to recognize anyone's speech in any language. Perhaps more important, it is becoming clearer with each passing day that the sheer force of new scientific breakthroughs is forging the peoples of the world into new kind of mutual cooperation, empathy and understanding. An intelligent, synergistic planetary civilization is now being birthed in an increasingly planetary society where the revered nation-state as we know it may one day largely disappear.

Over a hundred and fifty years ago Nathaniel Hawthorne said, "the world of matter will one day become a great nerve, vibrating thousands of miles in a breathless point in time creating a globe with a vast head and an intelligent brain!" About the same time, Samuel Morse telegraphed his immortal words, 'what has God wrought?' And if we pause to think about it, plenty of good reasons come to mind why humanity has been endowed with the incredible capacity for cosmic intelligence. The way we were made was no mistake and we'll find out why during this lifetime. We'll soon see the part of our brains we don't use finally unlocked.

Early in third millennium, because of the inevitable merger of television and the internet, 99% of the American population could be wired to the internet, allowing in just a few years the tapping into the sum total of the entire human experience including all the collective knowledge and wisdom that survived since recorded history began. Then, the so-called information highway, whose ultimate impact will be comparable to Gutenberg's first printing press, will no longer be a dusty, pot-holed back road but a smooth, super high speed race track made up not of merely copper wires, but sophisticated fiber optics with the power to easily transmit all of the Holy Bible or the Encyclopedia Britannica around the world to multiple sources in a fraction of a second.

However, unlike the quantum or computer or biochemical revolutions, the consciousness revolution, the age of spiritually based conscious awareness, is just beginning. We are all like little children who've finally learned to walk and are now just learning how to talk. Our neural connections and nervous system are mostly connected up and functioning well enough now for us to not only grab the rattle from the crib but toss it across the room. We're ready to climb out of our crib and start doing miraculous things, and it's the oversized brains we've been endowed with that will take us there, wherever 'there' is.

We know that the human brain contains 200 billion neurons, each of which is connected to 10,000 others which vibrate along at over 10 billion times per second —a confounding maze of parallel connections. The brain has the power to carry out trillions of operations simultaneously and uses no more energy than it takes to power one household light bulb. If a computer could be built as powerful as one human brain, it would need over 100 megawatts of electrical power. Modern computers can now calculate at nearly the speed of light but can handle only one calculation at a time. Our brains operate at the rate of trillions of calculations simultaneously and can even continue to function if part of it's destroyed or damaged. In some cases it can repair itself.

No doubt, computer power is today growing so

quickly there's no way to prevent the emergence of super-smart machines, but the big difference is that human brains know the meaning of things and computers can only follow sequential instructions, however advanced the program might be. Scientists face the daunting task of solving the fundamental problems of programming human consciousness, let alone self-consciousness. It may indeed be possible for humans to construct a thinking, conscious robot. When we do we'll probably welcome it and see it as being like our own child. It, too, will then come to be counted as one of the great multitude of creatures engaged in the continuous emergence of evolution on earth.

The fact is, most of us don't spend much time pondering philosophical questions about self-awareness, but rather we spend it puzzling out our own continuing survival and comfort. In the realm of artificial intelligence, however, experts say 'thinking machines' already exist. They refer to them as 'humans.' These same experts are trying to duplicate the human brain neuron for neuron. If they're successful, unnatural selection will have replaced natural selection. They're hard at work trying to engineer a thinking, even self-aware computer with an 'intelligence' superior to the human brain. Computer scientists say they will be able to make a machine that's smarter than us. They say humanity might then have to confront the notion of being superseded as a species. We'll see about that.

Is artificial intelligence (AI) simply an oxymoron or does it represent the Holy Grail? AI advocates say computers and the human brain are simply big information processing devices, and that one day they'll build a computer that surpasses the brain's calculating power. Some AI advocates say humanity in its present form is merely part of a rapidly passing stage of earthly evolution, simply a carbon-based life form. Our main purpose, they say, is to build a new species to succeed us, a species in a silicon-based life form. To believe otherwise, they contend, is just silly 'human chauvinism'.

Scientists tell us consciousness emerges naturally when any system becomes sufficiently complex and it simply arises out of the various interactions of many nonconscious systems. In humans, consciousness is spread out over many structures inside the brain; various parts simultaneously generate different thoughts that continuously compete for our brain's full attention. Consciousness, therefore, is not continuous but a succession of individual thoughts occurring in successive moments of now. For most of us, when we experience 'enlightenment' or true atonement (at-one-ment) it's only for a few seconds or minutes at a time. We get flashes of enlightenment and then it disappears, which explains why most experts say *full* consciousness has never been adequately explained because no one's been continuously fully conscious long enough to do it.

Until now however, no one has even given the world a widely accepted, definitive and compelling description of exactly what consciousness is. Without knowing, humanity continues to be drawn by some unseen force, being pulled inexorably toward the age of conscious awareness. We humans are determined to know our selves and discover our destiny. We won't take no for an answer so we continue without any fear of the unknown or where it might lead us. Like bears to honey, we are intuitively being drawn to something irresistible.

There is only one immutable 'law' in the universe, physical or otherwise that's recognized by all the other laws as being 'universal' and it's the law of evolution. Evolution dictates there are no flukes or historical accidents. There's a great deal of randomness and nature doesn't always take the simplest route toward its intended destination. It allows for gigantic changes to occur literally overnight and one of the end results is always consistent; evolution always produces some form of higher consciousness. This makes it highly unlikely that a machine could ever be made to be fully conscious and totally self-aware.

From a purely evolutionary perspective, plenty of evidence suggests that we who happen to be alive today are living at an extraordinary time in the overall scheme of things. We're at the epicenter of a period of constantly accelerating change that is virtually without precedent. And the beat goes on ever faster, speeding up more and more with every passing day. We need to think seriously about the implications of this. With accurate, instant, infallible and unencumbered planetary communications acting like the earth's own conscious control system, we'll soon have the capacity to begin functioning within a fully mature, synchronous, smoothly operating global matrix. Like a growing child suddenly able to think and act for itself, the quantum moment for the ultimate human/planetary transformational event will have arrived. It's going to happen! It can't be stopped. And it will happen 'in the twinkling of an eye, when we least suspect it', exactly as promised. Plan on it!

Since the 1960's the world has been increasingly blanketed with self-help and mutual help support networks and various motivational, personal success strategies. It's estimated over 100 million people worldwide are involved one way or the other in some kind of personal consciousness raising. Teachers, mentors and motivators in every imaginable spiritual and transformational discipline are busily going about raising people's awareness, motivating them to know more about their Creator, discovering themselves and their own life purpose. Soon the world will have 128 million times more information than when Jesus lived. These psycho-technologies of higher consciousness prove that increased awareness and spirituality are knowable and teachable through methods that are repeatable and measurable. Millions of people worldwide are now participating in the rapidly expanding field of consciousness raising and its effects continue to be felt in every corner of the world, while religious ministries continue their tireless, non-stop work, bringing spirituality, hope and the promise of a positive future to millions worldwide.

Today, by far the most dominant topics being communicated worldwide are spirituality and conscious awareness. They're being taught and discussed everywhere. For those wanting to expand their own personal consciousness, there are proven psycho-technologies for every taste and in every language. Even so, all of the various spiritual, motivational and transformational teaching methods now being offered barely scratch the surface of what's possible. It appears that the only limits to teaching higher consciousness, personal success and increased spirituality are in choosing how to best impart lasting thoughts effectively on a massive scale, in every language.

So, as evolution continues at warp speed with no signs of slowing down, it is not unreasonable to imagine the human race soon reaching a level where enough people come to think similarly and are able to instantly communicate enough congruent thoughts that a critical mass is created. Although no one knows exactly at what point critical mass takes place, when it finally does occur inertia will be overcome, momentum will begin feeding on itself and massive, positive changes will become the norm.

We should all be happy, not sad or depressed about this. Optimistic not scared, tranquil not irritated over where the world is headed. We're really doing quite well and we can certainly do a lot better. More and more people worldwide are working diligently at improving themselves and coming to know God so we should be happy. Make an effort to hang out with happy people who have discovered the path of their choosing and are traveling it.

We've seen that even though all of us function as

individuals, we're also similar to single cells functioning as part of a rapidly expanding, fully integrated worldwide living system. All of humanity and the magnificent earth we share are integral parts of this giant superorganism that lives and breathes and operates like a living entity with the ability to organize and self-regulate itself in various ways. Over-population may be the best example of a continuing problem we can be less concerned about because the natural forces of evolution are already working to naturally regulate it. Within the elaborate organizational structure of our living planetary home, the human population is right now in process of stabilizing completely on its own. So, while spaceship earth continues forward, humanity is busily fulfilling the prerequisites for an eventual breakthrough to a new and higher level of consciousness, whole-centered beingness and spiritual purity.

Our next level of consciousness will require the careful monitoring of the collective power and total intellect of humankind because it's completely illogical to think we'd be allowed to inherit the next higher plane as an immature, self-centered species. We'd be far too dangerous. We couldn't be trusted to use our power and intellect only for good and if we used it for evil we'd probably quickly kill ourselves off in no time. We can't be depended upon in our present state. Therefore, somehow, some way, we have to learn to surrender our self-centeredness. Unless we do we can't progress.

And we definitely are making progress. Everywhere we look at this moment, the world's people are consciously trying to re-organize themselves into an integrated larger whole, one that will ultimately work for everyone with no one left out and if our evolutionary past is prologue, it will come about in only one way: as a result of a giant leap to a new and higher scale of personal awareness and responsibility. We have not yet reached the point where we're ready for that and we won't reach it as a result of a man made physical or biological alteration or some social or political mandate. The cause will be much different and far more powerful.

All of this suggests a worldwide mental synthesis will occur, a meeting of the minds on a planetary level. Up until now every species has evolved to the next level together, all at once, not just some. Although many who cannot or will not adapt will certainly die when the next evolutionary leap occurs, every person alive will be profoundly affected. Because the results of evolution are consistent, we can be absolutely certain that all or most of humanity will have the opportunity to move into the next stage of evolution together or not at all. Successfully moving onto the next level will depend, therefore, upon a recurring evolutionary theme—the ability to become whole-centered beings rather than self-centered. Our self-image, our sense of a common identity and an enlightened collective vision for the future is what it is going to take. Our quantum instant of transformation is near. Be aware. Be sensitive. Behave.

The great transformation of humanity can only be truly realized when all the various communication links between humans expand to the point where trillions of signals create some kind of universally accepted planetary coherence. Then, because all human minds have been naturally programmed to constantly be on the lookout for any type of recognizable pattern, the planetary mind will eventually recognize a particular pattern similar to what the individual human mind knows and can acknowledge. This particular signal will silently drop into the consciousness of those who can accept it and trigger an evolutionary leap forward in human consciousness of an unimaginable magnitude.

Such an event is not only consistent with religious teachings, it's 100% consistent with natural evolution. Human history, like evolution, proves that things change only when they must and then only because of absolute necessity. Humanity is so stuck in its own narcissistic rut that most people can't imagine passing through an evolutionary shift to a higher level of consciousness where they see themselves as unique parts of a larger whole intelligent system and begin loving their neighbors as themselves. Still, that's what's in store for us.

What if it does happen and we all began functioning as one large, successful organism, the way other, smaller successful organisms function? A single cell cannot know the whole body even though it contains the design of the whole body in its nucleus. Still, each part could begin operating in harmony with one others in a deliberate effort to support one another and by doing so support the proper functioning of the whole system. In other words, working synergistically, the earth and everything on it would begin behaving as one giant living organism. Humanity would start functioning as the earth's brain and nervous system, supplying all the vital communications networks. Each person doesn't need to be a master of the whole design of creation or even fully understand it in order to play a vitally important part in making it work smoothly.

So, for us to begin seeing ourselves as one, we need to alter, adjust and fine-tune our own individual nature, in order to evolve more rapidly, inwardly more than outwardly. The great gift of self-awareness is the vehicle humanity will use to achieve this goal, so the most important changes in the future will take place within the realm of the spiritual and human potential movement. The on-going task of elevating human consciousness will take place one person, one mind at a time. That means we must all find a way within ourselves to summon up the willingness to pledge our allegiance to a higher cause. We must become whole-centered, God-centered human beings, fully aware of our own divinity. Otherwise we won't make it. We must surrender our self-centeredness to a mightier cause.

Chinese mystic Chuang-Tzu, living 1500 years ago wrote, "All in the universe including me are one when the self is given up." The Roman philosopher Plotinus observed, "When we stop being individuals, we raise ourselves ever higher and become able to penetrate the whole world." All spiritual teachings assert that we are all derived from the same source, so it's an illusion to see ourselves as separate from each other. We also see untold numbers of constituents in the universe which are all distinct, separate parts of a singular whole system, including various electric and magnetic forces—heat, cold, even time and space. It's the natural order of things for us to be the same and yet be entirely different. So, the time has come for us to learn to see our individual differences as a magnificent manifestation of our unique sameness for it is truly the source of all our power. It is the very God-force operating within and through each of us. We must all become more aware of it and purposely choose to become less self-centered in everything we do.

Hindus, who were practicing yoga 500 years before Christ, believe each child born is a God reincarnated. They believe when we die, our bodies return to the earth and our souls continue on. Could we all be part of a forgetful species that's in constant need of being reminded of our own natural divinity? It's time every person is reminded of their ultimate purpose and how magnificent we all are.

Virtually every scientific expert agrees on one point: there is some kind or type of unnamed ordering principle operating within the universe taking the form of perfect synchronicity in all things. Largely an unknown phenomenon, it functions not only in the physical world but also in both individual and collective human consciousness. Most people identify it as God. Others say it is the designing divine intelligence of the universe, a sort of cosmic creative global architect of everything. Others call it Nature and say it's essentially the randomness in the universe, responsible for both the cause and the effect of the natural order. Others describe it as the ever-present pulse of evolution. But by whatever name we call it, we did not invent it. *It* invented us and it has purposely positioned the whole of humanity at this particular time on the cusp of a monumental evolutionary leap. All who suspect or can intuit it are recognizing the signs all around us, signs slowly, steadily evolving right under our collective noses. For others, as was written in the Dead Sea Scrolls, 'they do not know the future mystery'.

A huge body of scientific and spiritual evidence now points directly at the very real probability that ours is the generation that finally will witness the end of a set of global trends that have been going on for thousands of years. It seems self evident therefore, that each member of the human race, one person at a time, must choose to change the way he thinks and operates or is destined to die off as a consequence of his own self-sabotage and self-destructive choices. Nature will see to it. The time has come for each of us to make the hard choices.

The world today is embroiled in a confrontational, confused and confounded mess almost everywhere we look. Socially, politically, financially, morally, spiritually and ecologically the world is in collective turmoil and seems to be breaking at every stress point. Civil and religious wars, racism and terrorism, nearly

20,000 children dead from starvation every day in a world of endless abundance, dread diseases inflict millions as mutating viruses rage out of control and worsen each day with no cures in sight. Violence, hatred and a death culture pervade much of the world. The world's gloom and doomers predict the final apocalyptic ending is imminent because they say never in the history of humanity have problems been so extreme and complex. Never before has humanity had as much power to upset the balance of nature as it does now. For these reasons we must all wake up! Shift our fundamental way of thinking. We must move away from our selfishness and work hard at learning a more holistic, whole-centered existence. However, without some sort of intervention, most people won't do that, so we can expect the catalyst that finally drives us to the end of the world to be consistent with the evolutionary process. We can expect to see more complexity and disordered instability until a certain limit is reached. Then we'll experience a very uncomfortable breakthrough. Until that incredible moment, the world will continue along 'at its petty pace' while the smart ones among us continue to expand their own spirituality.

Possibility thinkers are quick to see the problems in the world leading up to a positive rather than negative scenario for humanity, saying all these bad things are merely growing pains. And they're right. People today are much more consciously aware of themselves and their environment than ever. Millions of people are convinced that one day soon critical mass among the world's population will be reached and all of humanity will then be dramatically changed in a spiritually peaceful, constructive way, rather than in a strife-torn, destructive way. Because we have Free Will, the choice is ours. The continuation of our species depends on what choice we make.

We know that Nature's method of transformation has been operating through evolution since before life began and it will certainly continue operating when conscious evolution prevails and humans have at last become whole-centered, unselfish beings in a planetary society. Just as Neanderthal and Cro-Magnon man became extinct, so will our fellow humans who stay selfish and refuse to give it up their self-centeredness. As time goes on, the selection process will continue into a tribulation period where it will become even more closely defined until eventually a final selection will be made out of this stage of humanity's evolution. Everyone should be fully prepared for this event because no one knows exactly when the quantum instant will be upon us.

*The end will come like a thief in the night,*
*when you least suspect it.*

Thessalonians 5:2

# 9

# I Got Your Self-Awareness!

Thousands of years before Christ, Homo sapiens experienced a similar type of drastic transformation. A number of historians, archeologists and biblical scholars (not to mention UFO believers) point to what they say is convincing evidence that a life form from another planet long ago visited earth and populated it, us now being the cloned offspring of many generations past. Wild as it sounds, these advocates also insist that any day now our inter-galactic forefathers will return to earth to explain exactly how and why they created us, then they will move most of us onto the next level of existence alongside them. To the surprise of many, ancient writings abound which refer to this coming inevitability.

By way of explanation, most modern scientists agree that the first being on earth to be truly manlike in appearance—advanced Australopithecus—existed in Africa some two million years ago and it took another million years or so to evolve into Homo Erectus. It was 900,000 years later the first primitive man called Neanderthal put in his appearance and despite the nearly million years that passed from Australopithecus to Neanderthal man, their appearance and their tools and how they lived were almost identical. Then, all of a sudden and without any trace of where it came from, an entirely new race of people, Homo Sapiens—conscious man—appeared about 35,000 years ago.

Materializing seemingly out of nowhere, archeological evidence proves beyond doubt that Homo Sapiens must have been a fully conscious creature however, there's no evidence they were fully *self*-conscious creatures. That's a very big and important difference! Almost all traces of Neanderthal man's evolutionary advancement totally disappeared when these fully conscious men, referred to as Cro-Magnon and looking very much like humans today, took over. It wasn't until 25,000 years later, sometime around 14,000 years before Christ, that legitimate proof of the first truly 'self-conscious' or 'self-aware' humans appeared. It was as if some invisible and unknown designer had dispatched to earth a far better and infinitely smarter model to replace the original. It was clearly a very radical design innovation of truly immense significance.

It remains a continuing puzzle to this day why, over millions of years, early man survived by hunting and gathering food then suddenly became a farmer growing his own food. This was a monumental conceptual breakthrough. Obviously, man had to be fully self-conscious to do such work. Hard, scientific evidence proves conclusively that this extraordinary event occurred in what can only be described as an instant evolutionary flash in time.

And exactly where and when did this momentous

event occur? According to archeological evidence, the trail leads to a small Sumerian city in the Middle East called Eridu. Located in what was then southern Mesopotamia, Eridu is in present day Iraq, where today's eminent scholars agree that modern civilization, as we know it first began, about 14,000 years ago. Here, Homo Sapiens was suddenly and unexpectedly gifted with an unprecedented additional and most awesome power. Man was turned into a self-conscious, fully self-aware human being. No creature like it had ever existed before (on earth, anyway) and a radical, new civilization in Eridu instantly appeared out of virtually nowhere. It was a much more advanced civilization in many ways than all of the other ancient cultures that preceded it or followed it and it is without doubt the civilization upon which our own is founded.

Most interesting, to this day scholars have no idea where the Sumerians came from. There is no evidence whatsoever who they were or how such a new civilization could appear so suddenly, so totally unexpected and literally out of the blue. After hundreds of thousands and even millions of years of what was extremely slow evolutionary human development, scholars still cannot adequately explain this totally unprecedented transformation in humanity.

The Sumerians left prolific records and insisted that our solar system was made up of the Sun and twelve planets. Their written records of various astronomical calculations and drawings about inhabitants from this unknown twelfth planet intrigue archeologists and astronomers to this day. And for good reason! The Sumerians called this very special twelfth planet *Nefilim*; to them it was by far the most important of all the planets. They said it was the place from which their forefathers came and who promised one day to return! These ancient people of Sumeria charted the course of the planet of their origin, Nefilim, on its journey through the heavens. This despite most of the time its orbit remained outside of the earth's view, almost always hidden far away behind the sun.

The Sumerians described Nefilim and its behavior in the heavens in terms similar to those of a comet. It is widely known that some comets have been seen only once in human history. Kohoutek, for example, last seen in 1974, disappeared behind the sun and will not appear in the sky again for as at least another 7,500 years in an orbital path which remains outside of the earth's view almost all the time, hidden behind the sun. This also explains why today's astronomers know nothing substantial about Nefilim. Still, there is much speculation among today's astronomers about the apparent existence of some unseen 'planet x' which remains unseen and whose presence can only be proven mathematically as a consequence of the known gravitational affect it has on the orbital paths of other known planets.

Several books of the Bible and various Mesopotamian texts make references to this twelfth and mysterious planet. In fact, the anticipation of the Day of the Lord in Hebrew writings (and also in ancient Mesopotamian texts) was predicated on the periodic return of this special planet to the vicinity of the earth. The Sumerians planned for Nefilim to make its eagerly anticipated, periodic return precisely every 7200 years.

Sumerian writings insist that self-conscious man as we know it was created by the Nefilim, an assertion that at first appears to clash head-on with Judeo-Christian beliefs as well as the theory of evolution. But the truth is, Sumerian texts confirm both the theory of evolution and the Judeo-Christian beliefs. They explain that when the Nefilim first came to earth, the arts of farming, grain cultivation and fruit growing were virtually unknown. No sooner did the Nefilims arrive than archeological proof shows man began engaging in exactly those endeavors. However, we also know that self-awareness is not always accompanied by a highly developed civilization.

Not surprisingly, the bible also tells us when God first created Adam from dust, He assigned him to work in a garden called Eden. The biblical story of Creation, like many tales in Genesis, stems from Sumerian origins. Even condensing many Gods into one single Deity is of Sumerian origin. In the bible, the word 'Elohim' denotes Gods, God being a dual gender, plural word, e.g., 'Let us make man in our image and after our own likeness'. The first man (and woman) therefore, were created similar to God materially, emotionally, internally and externally according to Holy Scripture. Nowhere however, does the bible say the first man created was fully self-aware. But Adam was definitely fully self-aware and so was Eve.

Clearly then, Adam could not have been the first man ever on earth but he was undoubtedly the first fully self-conscious, self-aware human creature on earth with the gift of being able to understand the notion of God. Today, it is generally accepted by fully 25% of the world's people that the biblical Adam was purposely created and was the first fully aware, fully self-conscious man.

Evolution therefore, goes a long way to satisfactorily explain the course of events regarding how all life developed on earth, but evolution cannot and does not explain the appearance of Homo Sapiens, modern self-aware man, which came into existence almost instantly in terms of the millions, even billions of years of evolutionary history. So, if we are to accept only known evolutionary events, man definitely appeared millions of years too soon. Modern, self-conscious and fully self-aware humans apparently and obviously had to come about or be brought about in some other way, perhaps by the Nefilim. It is therefore reasonable and accurate to say that early man initially evolved, however, self-consciousness and self-awareness were uniquely supreme gifts from some outside source. For those believing in a fundamental overriding notion that God creates everything, God also created evolution in all its many forms.

Astronomical calculations of the Sumerian's orbital path of their mysterious twelfth planet coincides with countless other end time prophesies including the coming of the new astrological age, the age of Aquarius. The time for Nefilim's next scheduled reappearance near to the earth has been calculated to be sometime around the year 2000 when, they say, we should look for the sign of the water bearer, the symbol of the Age of Aquarius.

*Anybody who thinks the earth has been visited by space aliens is completely whacky!*

Clyde Clack

# A Visit to Camp Nirvana  10

Suppose somehow, some day humanity does evolve into the next stage of evolution into what has been described to us and called such things as Heaven, The New Jerusalem, Nirvana, et al. What can we expect? What might that ineffable state be like? Despite some people who claim to know about the subject through personal experience, it's really the ultimate exercise in trying to literally think the unthinkable. Nevertheless, we must at least try.

Imagine yourself being suddenly awakened to discover you now have the ability to see and fully understand that you've been divinely blessed through pure grace. You have a childlike feeling of being in the very presence of what you imagine to be the Almighty. You are feeling like an undeserving, even unworthy newcomer in this unusual and perfect space when you suddenly notice that you now have a beautiful, perfectly functioning body. You sense it was your fledgling faith that served as the irresistible magnet in your life which delivered you to this divine place, and now you can at last begin to function in a space of enlightened purpose and unconditional love. You sense an ineffable inner knowingness, explaining how the mysterious Godforce lovingly and silently communicated its ultimate design into everyone's heart! You are in a space where earthly death has no dominion and you begin actually feeling the gentle warming aura of the loving presence transforming you. You discover you have no fears or regrets. A breathtaking emotion engulfs you; it is the expectation of soon being re-united with your loved ones and even your pets and the extraordinary ability to intelligently communicate with them makes your senses overflow. You feel the wonder and excitement of being freed from your separateness from God and all of His creatures. Gone with it forever are your fear, anger, revenge, anxiety, jealousy and all your compulsions. You are free at last!

You will joyfully play and laugh with your lost beloveds, fully understanding telepathically that you are about to begin fulfilling your life's true ultimate purpose. The feeling of unworthiness fades when you again notice it was simply your faith and your willingness to change that brought you here. You see yourself with new eyes and are amazed to notice you're no longer earth-bound. You revel in this new space where there is no time and you bask in the total absence of all sickness, pain, suffering, sadness and loneliness. You now see that your time on earth was an apprenticeship which is now complete.

You know you'll soon become a conscious co-creator with God and become one of His contributing partners. It is only one more in an endless series of extraordinary mysteries which will be silently revealed to you. Somehow, deep down you already knew everything in this magical space as it continues to remind you of your past and future. You discover you possess the incredible power to select whether you are a creature made of matter or being composed of pure consciousness. And when you choose pure consciousness, you can easily and instantly travel immense distances across space even faster than the speed of light.

Never could you have ever imagined experiencing this level of clean, pure happiness, free from all worries, survival needs and disabilities. Now, for the first time, you suddenly become aware of everything that did not fulfill the will of God, did not survive and isn't here. Up 'till now you never fully understood God's love for you and you realize the irony that it was your own weak belief in God that had kept you from really knowing Him. At last you see His love manifested in everything and you suddenly realize that evolution and creationism are obviously His twin methods of transformation. His Kingdom now come, His will now done, you finally realize the constant mental force pulling at you, tugging at you your entire life was intended to bring you closer to the designing Creator.

A transcendent nerve deep within you confirms that the appearance of the former world with all of its unexplained randomness was not the ultimate nature of reality. Now you've come to understand it's God's will to grant intelligent life the unique gift of becoming co-creative with Him. You realize that your willingness to overcome past fears and surrender your self-centeredness was the basic energy that provided the force allowing you to be transmuted to this place. How grateful you are to see it has resulted in a far greater payoff than any vain attempt to sustain your former human condition. You're overwhelmed to be an integral part of the precious self-elect. Here in this space, with your senses filled with self-satisfaction in an unbroken state of supreme bliss, you are suddenly able to recall the time you were safely ensconced in your own Mothers' womb and you know that this space provides even more security and contentment. You recognize that finally you're mature enough to truly know your Maker and at last you've broken through the invisible barrier that has kept you separate.

You somehow know that all who are here with you represent far more than the sum of the individual selves. Everyone is under divine aegis and can do things together none could have previously accomplished alone. You thrill at discovering, as promised in the bible, that you can do all the things Jesus could do and much more. You can even be in more than one place at the same time. Now, having become a true member of the Kingdom, you fully acknowledge these extraordinary gifts, never imagining it could be this real. Your brainpower continues expanding, opening up to you the realization you're embarking on the greatest and most spectacular of adventures, all of which promise to be a never ending odyssey into the exploration of your own true potential. Magnificent, uncountable glories continue to be revealed to you as wisdom pours forth silently into your rapidly expanding brain.

You know this is all part of your birthright. It is a

fulfillment of your faith and at once you're emotionally overcome as a flood of tears cascades from your unbounded happiness. Then suddenly you notice the earthly flowers, trees and the vegetation all around you. You're reminded as if seeing them for the first time and you closely examining the brilliant, rich magnificence of the universal design. You now know deeply that each of the trillions of all living things were consciously and purposely created in a continuing process and you're eager to begin working alongside the others creating countless new things. Soon you will learn to create entirely new varieties of flowers, trees, vegetation, new and different animals, new fish and bird species and you realize that this new, self-chosen life as both the designer and the designed is now fully underway in a sacred space where all of God's promises and yours are fulfilled.

The ordering principle for everything in the universe becomes clearer to you and you come to fully know it for what it is; the cornerstone of the way all things are created. Your former lack of understanding disappears and you see clearly that this cosmic consciousness, this blissful contentment and ethereal connectedness always been available to you. Increasingly, your ability to love others as yourself becomes easier and natural. The truth dawns on you that it was solely your limited, even fragile faith that enabled you to be totally transformed from being humanly perishable to divinely imperishable.

Now, having become a pillar of the affirmation of truth, the promise of a real personal/spiritual existence far better than anything you could ever imagine virtually spellbinds you in the presence of the Divine. Now you know. His Kingdom has finally come, His will finally done on earth as it is in heaven.

*All that you are and all that you will be
is the result of all that you think.*

Anonymous

# The Ins and Outs of It 11

Every person who ever existed experienced the biological quantum instant in the moment he was born. We now await the inevitable planetary quantum instant and one thing is sure; that most memorable of all events is sure to be an epiphany for the self-selected on earth who, out of their own free will, shall be mysteriously moved onto the next level of spirit, a place of greater self awareness and far higher consciousness. Like it or not, it is the inevitable next stage in humanity's own historical evolutionary journey and you can count on it to happen in our lifetime. Mankind now possesses a body of evolutionary facts to support the notion that the world and all of humanity is about to undergo this massive evolutionary shift. We can expect it to be an event at least as great, perhaps greater than when life first appeared on the planet.

In the near future, we can expect to see those who impede the progress of humanity to slowly self-select themselves out as more and more people become guided by their inner sense that all humans are members of one planetary human body and our collective future is far more promising than it ever could possibly be as egotistical, self-centered individuals.

Meanwhile, when each of us moves from our unconscious evolution into a state of conscious evolution we will begin to develop a capacity to more clearly see the invisible hand of Nature and come to realize that unity and atonement (at-one-ment) is possible for all of us while we're alive. Furthermore, the instant that we chose it we begin to think and behave differently which allows us to then freely choose to be happy and loving knowing our happiness is not outside of us, waiting to be found, but deep inside us, where it has always been. All of us will then begin to tell the truth all the time with nothing added and nothing left out, naturally manifesting our natural integrity. We will begin to give up our old desires to punish our antagonists and instead begin to develop powerful relationships with others that truly work for all parties.

We've been told that religion, legend, mysticism and evolutionary science have all postulated the end of the world as we know it. However, to satisfy them all, many more prophesies must first be fulfilled before the onset of the last days and before the world's believers should really expect the reappearance of the Christ.

We've been told that in the last days we shall be entertained by highly paid athletes, that men will masquerade as women, that the world will lose its moral compass, children will disobey their parents and teachers, that bare breasted dancers will be commonplace, many new musical sounds will be heard, earthquake frequency will increase dramatically, wars and the rumors of wars will prevail accompanied by strange diseases and pestilence, women's power will be greatly increased and a Jew will become the last Pope. All of these prophesies and many more have come true except the last one. Interestingly, one Cardinal likely to be chosen Pope by the College of Cardinals is currently a high ranking Vatican official whose mother was a Jew.

Christ and others have told us the kingdom of God resides within each of us, a reference that clearly supports the notion that we are all one and everything is within us. That which is within is also without and vice versa. This awareness is not intended just for a few special enlightened ones, but is available to us all. It is everyone's birthright. Nonetheless, almost all humans still perceive themselves as 'in here' and the rest of the world 'out there', which has been precisely humanity's plight since time immemorial. With all of humanity irretrievably 'skin encapsulated', how can we begin to see ourselves as one and start behaving that way?

First of all, humanity has always wanted to improve conditions in the world without first giving thought to improving itself. For almost everyone, a true affinity with the world around us just isn't possible. We've all been blocked mentally by some unseen force, perhaps the biblical 'power of the prince of the air', which demonically wants to keep us from knowing ourselves as others. Try as we may, most of us cannot begin to experience a close affinity with more than a select few close individuals. But now, this continuing urge by so many people to expand their affinity to others and to all of nature is an indication the universe is trying to evolve to a higher synthesis through us.

Drawing upon the truths, insights and experiences of all those who have come before us ... the Saints and seers, mystics and religious teachers, scientists and astronauts as well as recent developments in chemistry and physics, biology, sociology and psychology, physiology, medicine and systems theory ... we have successfully proven to ourselves that each individual is an integral part of an evolutionary design that has been on going for billions of years. It's still ongoing and remains unstoppable.

Explicit underlying patterns demonstrating the consistent intelligence of nature provides us with powerful evidence validating the view that our future is filled with promise. Therefore, each of us has good reason to be looking forward to happiness and satisfaction, peace, love and fulfillment far beyond our wildest imaginations, not global doom, gloom and destruction. This comes from our knowing that an authentic worldwide transformation to higher consciousness one person, one mind at a time is well underway. It is truly humanity's greatest quest. The number of people presently involved in the consciousness-raising movement is doubling every two years or less, making it the single steepest growth curve the world has ever seen. It now occupies the attention of half of the English-speaking people in the world and soon the involvement curve for consciousness processing will overtake information processing. The evolution of human consciousness will become the leading field in all of human activity, signaling a clarion call to the end of the nuclear/ industrial/information age and the official beginning of the long-awaited *Age of Conscious Awareness.*

It's supremely important that everyone on the planet comes to realize that humanity is now poised on the cusp of an evolutionary leap which will occur in a split second flash of evolutionary time, a complete transformation so great that it occurs only once in a billion or more years.

Spirituality and higher consciousness are now as topical as laptops and have become the dominant theme talked about on the Internet, despite most people still having to push against the barriers of the old consciousness. As more and more people become involved in bettering themselves, it is sure to become easier for more and more to travel the road of self-discovery. And, since the primary purpose of all evolution is the emergence of higher consciousness, as more and more people raise their levels of consciousness, widespread synchronicity will naturally occur.

A quick look around the world shows that it's exploding with mental and physical self-improvement psycho-technology, many of which are loosely drawn from ancient spiritual traditions. We see such things as bio-energetics, Shiatzu, biofeedback and isolation tanks, hypnotherapy, autogenic trainings, Theosophy, Rolfing and Hellerwork massage, holistic medicine and health foods, Feldenkreis, Scientology, Silva, osteopathy and chiropractics, acupuncture, naturopathy and iridology. We have all sorts of therapies including

Reichian, sex, primal and dream, logotherapy, reality and gestalt. We've had re-birthing, arica, est, Esalen and Lifespring, Transcendental Meditation, the Forum, Visionquest and a myriad of sensitivity trainings, Eckankar, neurolinguistic programming and encounter groups, Rajneesh, Ram Dass, Deepak Chopra, psychosynthesis as well as psychodrama and androgyny workshops. People studiously practice t'ai chi, yoga, aikido, tantra and aura reading, tarot cards and astrology (the latter now shouting from the rooftops that for the last 2000 years the spring equinox has been in Pisces and has just recently shifted into Aquarius which, they say, is the age that will be characterized by extremely rapid spiritual growth.) The Church of Religious Science, Unitarianism, Scientology and the Science of Mind Church, along with many offshoots of the more traditional religious teachings offer proof of the insatiable appetite people have for expanding their personal consciousness. The Rosicrucians, Freemasonry and other secret societies... there seems to be something out there for everyone's taste, including a powerful variety of personal success and motivational seminars which appeal to individual fulfillment and goal attainment through intensive subconscious trainings.

Because we've been told we were created in the image of God, it seems logical that we must therefore have a very lofty purpose. Such vital feelings register in the human brain and are interpreted unconsciously by the mind as providing a fundamental sense of purpose to life. Spirituality, the name given to the emotion we all know when our primal sense of moral purpose is fulfilled, is an integral part of the ultimate human potential. We are all progressing from an unconscious to conscious evolution that allows us quick but infrequent glimpses of God's invisible hand. We've been told that regardless of our position in life, whether prince or pauper, beggar or king, famous or infamous, our purpose in this lifetime is to get ready for the next stage of our own evolution; to prepare ourselves for the time when we will be at one with our Maker, working alongside him as universal beings. On that day all humans shall be like angels. Then, the age of natural Christs will have officially begun.

Synergy is the watchword. It is Nature's way of producing results while also being the best way to turn others into useful, dedicated partners. We must therefore each become practical idealists by doing what works. Love is the only commodity that can possibly carry us there. We must finally choose to be guided by the knowledge that all of us are part of one body, and from this knowledge will come a deep-seated synchronicity sufficient to attract the unlimited power of Nature, instilling into all the strength to conquer any obstacle, no matter how large. Don't forget, this generation of which we are all a part is the first ever on earth to be aware of ourselves individually while also being aware of the whole. We do indeed have the power to create our own future.

*Destiny is not a matter of chance.*
*It's a matter of choice.*

S. Hawking

# What To Do About It  {}

Now comes the hard part. Actually getting ready for what's coming. For those interested in specific, crystal clear instructions for exactly how to prepare for the rest of your life, you can start by first realizing exactly how lucky you are to be alive at this particular time. Don't forget, as recently as 300 years ago nearly everyone in the world was illiterate; almost everyone lived a life we of today could not tolerate.

Back then very few people could even read. Throughout their lives, people seldom traveled more than a couple of miles from where they were born. Every day whether they were sick or not, they worked at back-breaking hard labor from sun up to sun down, just to get enough food to eat. Nutrition was terrible. Mere subsistent levels of food, clothing and shelter dominated daily thoughts. There was little or nothing in the way of entertainment or relief from their miserable existence and nearly everyone lived with chronic diseases and debilitating physical problems.

There was no such thing as toilet paper or personal hygiene products. Hunger and starvation were widespread. If your leg was broken, few could set it straight so you limped until you died. Very few people lived as long as forty. Pregnant women worked in the fields until their water broke and then they'd give birth. With no rest, they'd strap the baby on their back and go back to work. People died long, painful deaths and it was common for them to lose their minds, killing themselves rather than suffer from endless weeks of pain and suffering. An abscessed tooth, a kidney stone or a burst appendix was a long torture.

Make no mistake about it, our ancestors as recently as a hundred years ago demonstrated more pure bravery just getting through one single day than what's been required of most of us in a lifetime. Our forefathers passed through a survival of the fittest selection process damn few of us today could even hope to survive. Today, each and every one of us enjoys a quality of life infinitely better than any millionaire, King, Queen, Sultan or President who ever lived up until 50 years ago.

So it's high time we gave up all our petty, selfish complaints and began to appreciate how lucky we really are. Now it's time to start your own process of self-improvement for your own good by making the decision to be happy. Not just some of the time, but all the time, even when things are really lousy. It's more fun than being cranky and even more important, it goes a long way to producing the kind of results you want in your life. It takes no training or talent to be happy because regardless of the circumstances you already know how to do it. There's no new information. All you have to do is choose. It's that simple. It's not about age or education or looks or circumstances or money.

Happiness is not something 'out there' we must look or wait for. Happiness is 'in here.' It is not a place to get to; it's a place to come from. To be happy you must first choose to be happy. There's no mystery to it. In fact, you can choose to be happy even when you have every reason not to be. When you do, you can then sit back and watch your life begin to work. You'll enjoy seeing people wonder why you're always walking around with that silly grin on your face. Try it for a month and your life will never be the same again. You'll be healthier and every aspect of your life will improve.

Secondly, everybody already knows right from wrong, good from bad, lies from the truth, and how to be nice to others. We have the power to choose and we live with our choices, so make the choice to do good and stay out of trouble. You already know how to do that and circumstances don't matter. You can be in jail or live in a castle. Wherever you are, others are sure to provoke you. If you fall into that trap, you earned it. Learn to stop reacting like a stupid machine to things people say or do. Learn to control your response to things that come into your life. Take pride in how you act when things don't turn out the way you want them. Learn to give up always having to be right and needing to always have things your way.

Stop making other people wrong by reminding yourself that if you had the same circumstances in your life and the same forces operating in your life that other people have operating in theirs, you'd likely have the same point of view as they do. So be willing to get off of your strongly held opinions and start doing what produces the results you want with other people. Quit trying to change them. When you get angry, begin to recognize it as a choice point, an opportunity for you to choose right from wrong and re-focus on what you really want. Tell the truth all the time, especially when it's not comfortable.

Thirdly, practice being whole-centered. It's an illusion that the human family is separate and different from each other so start treating other people nicely without expecting anything in return. Deep down, you know that under the skin everybody's the same, so stop pretending to be different from others. Don't gossip or complain about anything to anybody unless the person you're complaining to can fix it. Be nice to all animals and help them along. When you do these things your life will begin to work better, the problems you've been putting up with will magically disappear, and you'll wonder why.

Here's some tough advice. If you're a woman, you must come to the difficult realization that in this day and age men are better at expressing power than women. This is why most women today create power and then usually give it to a man to express into the world. If a man expresses the power he's been given well and also acknowledges the woman as the source of it, she will provide him with all the power he will ever need to succeed. However, if he uses the power given to him wrongly or fails to properly acknowledge the source of it, his power will soon disappear because she will withdraw it. Therefore, a man without a woman has no power source and a woman without a man doesn't have the best way to express her power into the world.

If you're a man, you likewise must come to the difficult realization that the overall quality of your life depends upon the quality of the relationships you have with the women in your life, especially your primary partner. You must acknowledge women as the source of all your personal power. In fact, you must realize that any one woman is several times more powerful than any man and only women can create power. It's critically important for all men to realize that they neither generate nor possess any power other than what women freely give them. Therefore, for a man to keep the power flowing he must be willing to constantly acknowledge the women in his life as the source of his power. This is every man's key ingredient for success.

Another important thing to learn is how to visualize the ideal life you want in exceedingly fine detail. Imagine it exactly the way you want it in every area, never limiting your visualizing to what you think is possible. Visualize without any limitations every day. Keep what you visualize to yourself because if you tell others, chances are most will try to talk you out of what you've visualized.

Do these things and you will provide yourself with all the energy and power you need to achieve the full potential that lies within you. No matter the troubles you may have in your life, remember you have not been forsaken. No one has ever been forsaken and neither has any one or any thing ever been damned. There's so much to live for nowadays with the magnificent mystery that's coming straight toward us, the final payoff for all the hurt and misery and meanness you've ever suffered at the hands of others. You have the solemn promise of a personal transformation in your lifetime. All that's necessary for you to do is what you already know how to do; choose to be good to others and choose to be happy all the time.

Finally, the most vital thing to do is begin knowing your own consciousness. This is because consciousness is in everything, everyone and everywhere. When you discover how to be conscious of being conscious you will be free to choose what to believe, what to think, how to feel and behave. You will then realize that you are what you think and you'll discover that your life is a result of what you think. Like it nor not, you'll see that you create your own world with your thoughts. Change your thoughts and your behavior changes. Change your behavior and your world changes. All thoughts cause a vibration which affects the entire cosmic vibration, so to have true mastery in life, you must come to know that controlling your thoughts is the way to create whatever reality you want in your life.

Harmonizing your consciousness with the universal consciousness will enable you to discover how to build the life you always wanted. You will quickly become fully capable of creating your own reality and perhaps for the first time in your life, take control of your circumstances. You will then come to see for yourself how to control all aspects of your life. This power is your birthright. All you have to do is claim it. All you have to do is recognize it, understand it and apply it. When you do this, you will instantly see that your emotions and your actions are always determined by your choices.

The choices you make determine the results you produce and you're responsible for it all. This is the great secret of human power and creativity. How you choose to think and believe and the action you take is what creates reality. Believe it or not; so be careful what you think.

Your external world is a direct reflection of your inner thoughts. What you think is within your control. Your power to choose is within your control. Your power to act is within your control. Once you have developed an understanding that all real power lies within you and once you've developed the ability to access and claim this power, you will find that the events and circumstances of your life are all directly under your control. Then you will have learned the real cause of all things in your life.

Every thought is a cause and every condition or circumstance an effect. This is what makes it abso-lutely essential for you to learn to control your thoughts. Your personal power is determined by just one thing: how tuned in you are to your real inner self.

Your future is entirely within your total control, always has been and always will be! Learn about yourself and the way you think. Think about how you think.

Notice what you think, what thoughts fly through your head.

Remember, you're in charge of all your thoughts. You're also in charge of all your actions and their results. If you don't like your life, change the way you think.

God wants you to be happy.

*If God came to you and asked you to
do something, you'd do it and be happy doing it.
The fact is, God has asked you to do something.
So do it and be happy!*

Werner Erhard

# In Defense of the Way Things Are

**12**

Randomness certainly exists in the world and sometimes things come into our lives accidentally and for no apparent reason. What really matters most is not the event itself, but how we react to it.

About 300 years before the birth of Christ, there lived a philosopher named Epictetus who taught that personal integrity was more important than material gain. This was a radical response to a world he saw as supremely self-centered and without morals. He taught followers that the entire universe, despite its apparent chaos and cruelty, is perfectly rational. All of its continuous unfolding events are intelligently pre-determined. All things that have ever happened, he said, happened exactly the way they were supposed to and to prove it, they did. He was a practical idealist. He was the epitome of an ideal that is known today as Stoicism. A slave born in the eastern part of the Roman Empire, he was a respected teacher who believed that what happens to us in life isn't what's important. What matters is how we respond to it.

He said, "things don't hurt us and neither do other people. It's our attitudes and reactions that cause us trouble". He taught that each of us can always be in complete control of how we respond to things even though we can't control our circumstances. "When bad things come into your life," he said, "don't make them worse by your own actions".

Epictetus said he knew nothing about such things as an afterlife but personal divinity could be attained by virtually anyone if they were only willing to exercise full control over their strongest passions and by acting rationally at all times, under all circumstances. This, he said, would allow anyone to walk on a strictly moral path in right relationship with all others.

Epictetus spent most of his life in prison and it was there that he realized his problems came not from the circumstances that entered into his life but how he reacted to them. It was this simple realization that transformed his life and the lives of millions after him. 'Things are the way they are,' he said, 'trying to change them only creates resistance. Persistence causes resistance and vice-versa.' One of Rome's kindest and most civilized emperors, Marcus Aurelius became a follower of Epictetus' teachings and Zeno of Citium even started his own school in a tent-like structure (or *stoa*) in Athens' central market area. Stoic teachings continued to greatly influence the early Christian patriarchs for nearly six hundred years after Christ.

Intellectual snobs, thinking life must be much more complicated, quickly dismiss such teachings as being absurdly simplistic, but a growing number of others, particularly those who have spent long terms in jail or as prisoners of war, easily recognize how they complicated their own lives while they were incarcerated by responding to circumstances in ways that only made their problems worse. As a slave, Epictetus knew that resisting authorities only made things worse for him, so he trained himself to always stay focused on the result he wanted to produce for himself. He dedicated himself to always behave in ways that would produce the result he wanted. He did not see this as surrendering but as simply doing what worked best.

Being in prison is no place for the weak of heart and Epictetus taught fellow prisoners to not let jail change them, reminding them that they probably earned their way in and now they must learn to earn their way out. The ancient creed of Stoicism allows those who practice it to maintain a high level of personal integrity, despite torture and isolation, because it allows the person to stand back and separate his emotions from things he cannot change. When things are seen that way, emotions evaporate and appropriate responses become easy. A certain freedom comes to the individual who gives up trying to change things that can't be changed. The person can then re-direct their energy toward what works. What then begins to emerge is the person's true purpose in life.

For most people, their real purpose lies deep within them; the vast majority of people, unfortunately, never discover it.

*We can't control what comes into our lives,*
*only how we respond.*

Epictetus

# The Next Chapter

The unleashing of humanity's full potential is a distinctly western idea and appears nowhere in the teachings of any of the eastern religions, Hinduism, Taoism or Buddhism. However, the most powerful religious institutions on earth are unquestionably Islam, Christianity and Buddhism. In fact, at least half the art and philosophy of humanity have been heavily influenced if not largely shaped by those three theologies and their creators, Mohammed, Jesus, and Buddha.

Buddha was an ordinary Hindu, Mohammed a lowly camel-driver and Jesus a simple carpenter. They shared no theory of any afterlife, no common doctrine or particular ethic, but they did share the same fundamental life identity. Somehow, some way, each of them had 'found out' how and why the world was organized as it is. Each of them predicted there would come a day when the last generation would die, but not until after all of humanity had learned the fundamental lessons; the essential knowledge of the differences between good and evil. Unlike other men, they were not ignorant of the nature of their own beingness, nor were they unaware of their own extraordinary powers. They made their lives a crusade to teach others the unseen truths they had discovered, telling them the world was governed by very different forces than what was popularly imagined. They encouraged their followers to work hard at becoming more spiritual, learn about themselves and to then fully express it into the world.

Our world has not had very many examples of highly evolved humans. Those we've had seem to have possessed the unique ability to experience a mental state of neurosomatic peace within a kind of hidden brain circuit which all humans are born with but few ever learn to access. Enlightenment, like every personal experience, is learned. Tapping into this particular brainwave is exactly what all of humanity is slowly and sometimes painfully learning to do. We are essentially progressing and evolving beyond our basic primate survival emotions to post hominid peace, ultimately out of the man-state and into the superhuman. It is inevitable. It will happen in this generation.

However, at this time in the history of humanity, the entire world civilization continues to behave like a spoiled brat. We are self-centered in most of our actions, easily angered, quick to cheat, steal and then lie about it. We are jealous of others, hold grudges, seek revenge and retribution. We immaturely act up in wild temper tantrums, wanting more than our fair share. These obviously cannot be the characteristics of the planetary civilization beyond this one. That one will surely demand an extremely high degree of cooperation among all its peoples.

When we look at today's world, we see it still plagued by deep fractures with cruel nationalistic, sectarian and racial animosity almost everywhere. So to advance out of this world into the next level of civilization where the complete secrets to all life and the atom will become scientifically and spiritually revealed to us, we cannot expect to drag along any of our old self-centered destructive baggage. Those purely human characteristics are obviously inconsistent with the immortal nature of a universal species. In the next world don't expect to see sniping, bickering people or nations still deeply separated along political or cultural lines. It won't happen.

The fact is, mastering interstellar space travel with space arks able to travel light year distances in seconds as depicted on television, however unthinkable today, will occupy much of our attention. To explore and colonize space, develop fully conscious artificial intelligence devices complete with learned feelings like Star Trek's Data character (which can repair itself), manipulate the weather, bend time, enter and pass through black holes, and move from galaxy to galaxy and even into and through other universes entertains our minds in a truly wondrous way. It dwarfs anything that is even remotely conceivable at present but the social and scientific demands of such an existence are totally inconsistent with self-centered creatures. To even begin seeing any civilization as advanced as those in the imaginary Star Trek and Star Wars type shows still living with today's self-centered human characteristics is truly absurd. When the present world as we know it passes away and the self-selected move on, our former destructive, self-centered characteristics must also disappear. Otherwise there cannot be a successful advancement. The natural course of evolution will make sure of it. The advanced features of the ultrahuman are certainly why the original title of the film "Revenge of the Jedi" was changed at the last minute to "Return of the Jedi." The Jedi, as we know, are highly evolved creatures who certainly know all about the human emotion we call revenge but they would never think to exercise it. Bottom line, humanity cannot and will not be allowed to move into the vastly more civilized world after this one until and unless we are willing to become pure of heart. To exist in space, humanity must become a planetary society, and that requires a complete letting go of our ingrained self-centeredness.

We can see this at work in the world today. We see all around us enormous increasingly visible pressures to create a truly planetary civilization, which must eventually include a global economy. The idea of nation states has served the world well; however, they're not an evolutionary constant, much less an eternal, sacrosanct concept. Nations were formed partly out of the basic belief in scarcities common to all humans. For centuries, there weren't enough of the truly valuable things in life to go around, like food and natural resources, so boundaries were erected and vigorously defended. It's only recently that humanity has begun to see that food is no longer in short supply, starvation in the world is no longer an inevitability, and solutions do exist. The only thing missing is the political will to end it. Likewise, viable and inexpensive alternative energy sources will soon be revealed to us. Today, more than ever, we see groups of nations coming together in various ways to handle mutual concerns.

The biggest obstacle to the notion of a planetary society lies with the political and military power of nations. One way or another, even this will be ultimately be settled as the world rapidly moves towards organizing itself in a way similar to the neurons in the human brain, each of which is separate, yet all sharing a common purpose. So, while erasing a long list of barriers separating us may not be an easy or a pleasing concept to many, it's an obvious necessity, integral to the natural order of things.

So the eternal question remains: what is the final destiny of all intelligent life? It is a soon-to-be transformation of ourselves from earthly ignorance and isolation into a loving galactic existence as newborn children of the stars under the aegis of the Godhead. Earth will continue to be our ancestral home. It is sure to be a mind-bending experience, a never-ending odyssey through curved space and parallel universes where we'll be introduced to the dizzying tenth dimension. We will come to know the nature of Nature and travel far faster than the speed of light without violating relativity. We will come to fully understand how and why the earth and all the planets move, what it is that pushes them on their orbits without being touched. We will know the geometry of space-time and finally come to recognize gravity and death as merely illusions. We will know about all of Nature's fundamental forces and when we look down on our former celestial home, the majestic planet earth, we'll finally understand it fully, completely and see it for what it is ... a four-dimensional space-time continuum. At that instant we will come to know the truth of everything spiritual, philosophical and theoretical. At that magic moment we'll be gifted with the breathtaking ability to read the mind and the divine will of God. There will no longer be any loose ends, no questions, no what if's.

We'll fully understand the uniqueness of the 'nothing' which existed before the Big Bang in no space, no time, no matter and no energy. We'll come to know the scientific principles and immutable laws governing the universe.

We'll know all about the Quantum Principle in the universe, explaining why there must always be uncertainty, while even nothing is always unstable. We will understand how our universe, like all universes, was at one time so tiny it could only exist in a minuscule, ghostlike, subatomic particle. We will understand how multiple universes were created in a million different directions on purpose and see exactly how they perfectly link together the story of Genesis with the ethereal Buddhist notion of Nirvana in the timelessness of eternal space.

It has recently been agreed among experts that all the physical constants of our universe exist now and always have existed inside a very limited bandwidth. Over eons, if those constants were altered in any way, chaos and instability would have instantly taken over, making life on our planet impossible. Called the Anthropic Principle, it has caused some scientists to argue that the makeup of our universe is the result of a bizarre, quizzical coincidence, an accidental, very fortunate fluke. Other equally esteemed scientists argue that it proves beyond doubt the existence of a divine cosmic Providence that continues to direct the fundamental ordering principle of the universe. These same people believe our own universe is different from all the others and was, somehow, purposely brought about in a way which created all types of life so that eventually a universal higher consciousness could one day arise.

Do we know more about the nature of the universe than we do the nature of our own being or our own spirituality or how our brains function? Most people have bought into the limitations of theoretical boundaries as to what humans truly are and what they can become. All of humanity is laboring under self-defeating, limiting superstitions which, of course, sound perfectly reasonable to the people who believe them. This is why it's so critically important that each person now alive embark on a voyage to discover more about themselves and how their mind works. Most people however, have an overwhelming resistance to doing this until they do and then want to kick themselves for not doing it sooner. Learning about oneself is a truly wonderful voyage that never ends. And the best part is it's all about you! What could possibly be more interesting?

All that's necessary is to open up your mind to some new possibilities, however strange they may seem at first. Once you learn how to locate the source of your own soul and discover how to tap into it and converse with it, your life will forever be better. Everyone has a soul inside their brain. In Tibetan Buddhism it's referred to as the White Light of the Void. Hindus call it Shiva-darshana. It's wu-hsin, the 'no mind' in China. At its core, your soul represents more than merely your individual essence; it represents your individual essence finally made fully aware of itself!

Each of us can learn to talk to this supremely important part of our brain. In fact, unconsciously we already do in a primitive way when we engage in 'self-talk'. We carry on a non-stop conversation with ourselves all the time, every waking hour, however; few people know how to do this properly and effectively. Most people's self-talk is simply a mindless exercise of self-centered random thoughts running on like a broken tape recorder. Little do they know that their self-talk is the brain's secret sub-conscious mechanism that creates almost 100% of what they call reality. Most people unwittingly access this self-talk mechanism in their brains with no idea how powerful it is and then proceed to confuse it with conflicting messages, unknowingly self-sabotaging themselves and wrecking their dreams. Worst of all, it never occurs to them to shut up and listen to what this extraordinary brain circuit has to say.

To successfully pass from this world into the next,

we must continue to become better at accessing and listening to this supremely important brain function. It lives in a section of our brain that never sleeps and when we learn to access it, it will automatically act like a super-conscious mirror that reflects everything while it silently directs our own intuition. It also throws open wide the wondrous gateway for introducing and becoming truly comfortable with one's own unique spiritual nature.

The best way to do this is under the instruction of a truly competent mentor in a well structured progam.

Make this your personal quest!

*... And when you have finally
reached the mountain top,
then you shall begin your climb.*

Kahlil Gibran

# So What's Next?

Author Marilyn Ferguson describes the world being on the verge of entering into a 'great shuddering, irrevocable shift—a turnabout in consciousness in critical numbers of individuals, a network powerful enough to bring about a radical change in our culture.' She writes about a 'new age' being upon us, a term used pejoratively by many religious groups. It simply refers to a new way of thinking that treats the whole of higher consciousness and spirituality as essentially related. But the 'new age' also refers more specifically to the near term transfiguration of humanity which the Hopi call the Great Day of Purification when the forces of light will overcome and finally prevail over the forces of darkness; a time of collaboration and cooperation among all the world's peoples that releases powerful forces of love, creativity and wisdom.

We've been told that whenever an 'age-change' takes place, Avatars or teachers are sent among the people to prepare them by radically altering the way they see things. Age changes occur approximately every two thousand years and the last time one occurred, Jesus came to teach truths which altered people's thinking forever. At this time thousands of lesser Avatars are among us everywhere, teaching spirituality, self-discovery and personal success.

The so-called new age soon to be upon us requires important work to be done. It will be a time when everyone's true motivation for spiritual work will be severely tested for its purity, a time when everyone must take total responsibility and become re-born as spatial citizens on earth, able to pour out a never-ending stream of unconditional love telepathically. It will be a time when science learns how to convert electromagnetic energy into the power required to travel long distances in space. Einstein's Unified Theory will finally be complete and we will no longer be earthbound creatures limited just to this planet. The toxicity and poison of humanity's past earthly living will be thoroughly cleansed and we'll finally see everything clearly for the first time. We will recognize our earth as a sacred planet, our ancestral home.

Some may continue to insist the earth cannot be seen as a living object. Others may deny the theory of evolution, while still others say that most scientific thought is simply the result of a short-sighted education in advanced tunnel-vision. However, the facts are just the opposite. We know now that the earth and everything on it is unquestionably moving rapidly toward its inevitable rendezvous with Nature, so now is a time of utmost importance in the evolution of mankind's spirituality as well as the planet itself.

The Bible clearly tells of a time when the earth will pass through a period of great turmoil and into a new age, a time of unimagined peace and good will. Evolution today is universally accepted as fact, not fiction. Science continues to find its most amazing discoveries through validations of long known, respected spiritual truths. As humanity is finally finding out, there are no such things as miracles, only what's so.

William Shakespeare called the earth 'this pendant world' and one day very soon everyone will see it for what it is...the stage upon which we all strutted our human drama for thousands of years. This magnificent third planet out from its parent star will then be seen as only one of many planets with previously unseen life swarming all over it just waiting to be explored and nurtured by us.

We now know that Nature's on-going task is to transform all existing life into new and improved models. Everything that now lives on earth is forever anchored to that idea and is therefore the result of all the forces and influences on it. It's getting easier for everyone to see how the vigor of our planet is linked. It's therefore incumbent upon man to look within himself and listen carefully for instructions on how to properly behave in relation to the planet as well as to others and to himself. It's foolish for anyone to be afraid of the future and just as foolish to be apathetic. We must be willing to learn how to survive the coming events in physical and emotional balance.

The choice is ours. We can either look upon the coming tribulations as only trouble and grief and there will certainly be plenty of that. The truth is, it's also going to be a time that brings welcome relief to the struggles of millennia past which at last will finally be over. On that majestic day there will be a releasing of an enormous negative pressure which has blanketed the world and stifled creativity since the dawning of time.

We are all like cosmic pilgrims, children of destiny. None of us can simply quit the process of finding out how the universe is organized and what our purpose is in it. The Spiritual Hierarchy of the universe has been bombarding our planet with its vastly increased cosmic intelligence for one single purpose: to rapidly increase individual consciousness. It is doing this in hundreds of disparate ways and everyone is on a different rung of the spiritual ladder. It's the obligation of everyone to assist one another in expanding their self-awareness and by doing so better understand themselves.

We must all continue to nurture our will to live and look upon any feelings of despair and defeat in a positive way. We must all somehow gather up the willingness to put forth the effort required to stay positive. It's a test we must pass in preparation for what is soon to be the severest test of our lives. We can no longer afford to be victimized by our own laziness. We must be well acquainted with all the various prophesies and know the warnings and promises they represent.

Be aware of the dangers of the times we live in and take proper precautions. Keep a positive, constructive, high-toned attitude all the time, especially when things are difficult. Some of the truest things in life you cannot prove, but you can still know and honor them. So remember you have a definite purpose in the scheme of things even if right now you're not sure what it is. Become comfortable not knowing and try to intuit your role within the Divine plan unlimited by what you think is possible. Be sensitive to all things around you, knowing that everything is involved in the great cosmic dance of life.

Be solid in your personal belief systems that work for you. Think about the timeless, continuing unfolding of the divine plan and commit yourself to staying aware. Stay conscious at bringing balance to the karmic state now in the world. Be extra sensitive to the pulse of the general population and assist people in moving through it. Meditate or pray at least twenty minutes every day. Practice deep breathing. Exercise and stretch. Know that you can stave off doom and gloom scenarios purely by your own intention. Be sure to support the earth as it works to fulfill its own divine evolutionary task. Never forget that everything on earth is the result of God's on-going intention to bring His ultimate vision for us into being. Each of us are a part of that sacred web, so be quick to give thanks. Be grateful. Have fun, laugh a lot, and dream your dreams with confidence in the future.

The end of the world and what to do about it? Since it's going to happen in our lifetimes, learn to take charge of all your thoughts. Every thought weaves the web of your reality. Practice expressing your love, because when you do your heart vibrates at the same rate as the earth and puts out far more electromagnetic vibrations than even your brain can generate. Because God's universe is truly a mountain of love, you will find yourself existing in eternal sustenance.

Lastly, each of us can galvanize our own personal security for the future only by discovering what our individual role is in the unfolding universal age. The only way to ascertain that is through the age-old process of self-discovery. There is no other alternative. As each of the coming massive earthly changes take place, people will respond differently, some rationally and others not.

Hopefully, dear gentle reader, simply as a consequence of having read this book, you will be better prepared than most.

# About the Authors

## Medard Gabel:

Mr. Gabel is the Executive Director of World Game Institute, Inc. a twenty-six year old not-for-profit research, planning and education organization that fosters responsible change and citizenship in a global society. Based on the pioneering insights of Buckminster Fuller, the Institute today is a non-governmental organization officially sanctioned by the United Nations that develops tools and techniques for recognizing, defining and solving global socio-economic problems and local problems in a global context. It has developed computer software, databases, and a wide variety of educational materials, research and experiential workshops for government, corporate, academic and general public markets throughout the world. Its clients have included AT&T, Astra-Merck, Bell South, Chase Manhattan Bank, Cigna, Du Pont, Exxon, General Motors, Glaxo, Motorola, Microsoft, Rohm & Haas, the World Bank,YPO, the Japanese Junior Chamber of Commerce and over a thousand universities and colleges throughout the world.

Medard Gabel has written four books on global problems, planning methodology and the U.S. food system. Energy, Earth and Everyone, the first edition of which was published in 1975, was the worldís first comprehensive inventory of the entire planetís renewable energy resources; it also presented a series of regional plans and a global plan for phasing out nuclear and fossil energy use and making the transition to a renewable energy based hydrogen economy. Ho-Ping: Food for Everyone, was the first comprehensive inventory of the entire planetís food production capacities and the possibilities for sustainable agriculture to meet the growing food needs of the entire world; it also presented a series of regional plans and a global plan for phasing in a sustainable food system that eliminated famine, hunger and malnutrition. Empty Breadbasket, examines the problems of the U.S. food system and what can be done about them at the farm, national and state government, research and consumer level. In addition, Mr. Gabel has published numerous articles on food, energy and planning in a variety of journals, magazines and books.

Mr. Gabel has also directed the development of three computer software applicationsóan interactive atlas program called Global Recall, a statistical data base program called Global Data Manager, and the Internet-based global simulation NetWorld Game. All three are in use throughout the world. He has also participated in the design and construction of a number of museum exhibits that are in use at the St. Louis Science Center, Franklin Science Museum in Philadelphia and the Connecticut Science Center.

Mr. Gabel has been a consultant to the U.S. State Department, Department of Agriculture, Energy, USAID, the governments of Tanzania, Costa Rica, and the Netherlands, the Governor's Energy Council of Pennsylvania, Congressman Robert Edgar, and the Food Task Force of Philadelphia. He has lectured and given workshops at over one hundred universities, including, Harvard Business School, Yale, Princeton, and the Universities of Pennsylvania, Colorado, and Southern California. He is a past member of the Board of Directors of the Pennsylvania Energy Development Authority.

Mr. Gabel regularly conducts workshops on globalization for executives from Motorola in their Global Institute for Managers and for various divisions of General Motors. He has also delivered similar programs to executives at British Airways, Du Pont, Cigna, Astra-Merck, Chase Manhattan, AT &T, American Express, BellSouth, CompuServe, Batelle, ChemAbstracts, OCLC, Detroit Edison and over 20 other corporations.

# Hugh Jeffries:

Born near Buffalo, NY, Hugh Jeffries attended secondary schools in Connecticut. He married his high school sweetheart, Dotty Lloyd, in *1957*, completed four years at the University of Harford in three years, was elected President of the honorary fraternity and received a degree in business. He formed an insurance agency with Travelers and subsequently sold it to Alexander & Alexander (AON). When he and his wife moved to California in 1969 where he became a writer and producer at Universal Studios. He formed his own company in 1975 to write and produce TV commercials, promotional/training films, music videos, political media campaigns, documentaries, and a wide variety of work in the personal achievement and human potential movement. His award-winning work has taken him to 28 countries on five continents.

A member of the Screen Actors Guild and AFTRA, he has also been active on various television programs *(7th Heaven, melrose Place, HBO and Showtime Comedy specials)*. A former network announcer, he has also appeared in numerous TV commercials and is active as a voice talent. Represented by The Lloyd Group, Burbank, CA, Coast to Coast Talent, Hollywood, CA and Cavalieri & Associates, Burbank, CA, he is managed by Felice Gordon. Contact The Lloyd Group (818) 566-1095 for a complete list of credits. e-mail: hjeffries@ earthlink.net.

## Leslie Fieger

Leslie Fieger is the founder of DELFIN International Inc., a company dedicated to Transforming the Way the World Thinks. He is the author of "The DELFIN Knowledge System", a best-selling trilogy of personal empowerment self-study programs sold worldwide by independent distributors.

Leslie is a charismatic public speaker who has enlivened thousands of people about human potential, freedom and self-reliance. Seminars are conducted in the world's finest accelerated teaching environment, a high-tech multi-sensory program that enhances intelligence, creativity, retention and application.

He resides primarily in the Carribean with his partner and scuba diving buddy, Sandra Hartley, and together, they travel the world conducting seminars and exploring the ocean's depths.

He plans to survive the end of the world.